To Dad.
Happy Christmas 1988.

love as always

Mag. X.

STEAM
ALL THE WAY
Nigel Harris

WHSMITH
EXCLUSIVE
·BOOKS·

FRONT COVER: The last main line steam locomotive to be built for British Railways, Riddles Class 9F 2-10-0 No. 92220 *Evening Star* evokes memories of 'The Pines Express' at the head of a train of BR-liveried maroon coaches, shortly after leaving Grosmont, on the North Yorkshire Moors Railway, on April 19, 1986. *Peter Zabek.*

REAR COVER: Southern Railway 4-6-0 No. 850 *Lord Nelson*, painted in eye-catching malachite green livery, approaches lonely Ais Gill Summit, on the Settle-Carlisle line, with the southbound 'Cumbrian Mountain Pullman' of March 3 1984. *John Cooper-Smith.*

PREVIOUS PAGE: London & North Eastern Railway 'A4' class 'Pacific' No. 4498 *Sir Nigel Gresley,* named after its designer, speeds past Cross Gates, near Leeds, with 'The West Yorkshire Enterprise', a Leeds — Hull special working of September 22 1984. Sister locomotive No. 4468 *Mallard,* preserved as part of the National Collection, holds the world speed record for steam traction, of 126mph, established in 1938. *Peter J.C. Skelton.*

THIS PAGE: No. 5593 *Kolhapur,* one of the London Midland & Scottish Railway 'Jubilee' 4-6-0s designed by Sir William Stanier, is pictured at Henley-in-Arden on June 8 1985 with 'The Shakespeare' Express'. This locomotive is based at the Birmingham Railway Museum, Tyseley. *Mike Esau.*

INTRODUCTION

ALTHOUGH everyday steam traction on the railways of Great Britain ended after nearly 150 years in August 1968, the 'iron horse' is still surprisingly active today. There are about 100 private railways, museums and steam centres throughout the country, housing around 1,000 standard gauge steam locomotives, including around 450 former British Railways locomotives, and 550 former industrial shunting engines. Some locomotives are polished as non-working museum exhibits, whilst others work regularly each year, hauling passenger trains over private tracks varying in length from a few hundred yards to more than 20 miles. Some main line locomotives still work at up to 60 mph over British Rail routes, with special excursion trains. Steam is still very much alive.

The steam engine has always been a popular subject for the railway photographer and *Steam All The Way* is a celebration of the examples we can still see today, especially those still at work. Many different types can be seen, from former main line express to the fussy little goods yard tank engine, and this book covers a wide range. It would be impossible to mention every preserved locomotive, or tell the definitive story of the steam locomotive from 1825 to 1960 within the covers of a single volume, and *Steam All The Way* does not pretend to do this. Concentrating on standard gauge locomotives only, this book traces the basic evolutionary thread of the main line express steam locomotive from the last quarter of the 19th century to the introduction of the BR 'Standard' classes, following Nationalisation in 1948. The text describes how locomotives grew in size and power to keep pace with increasing train weights and faster schedules, and uses selected preserved locomotives to illustrate general trends and developments. This book is designed both to give the reader an overall impression of the evolution of the express steam locomotive, and to sketch in background detail of selected interesting survivors. Chapters 1-4 outline this development, whilst Chapters 5-8 cover mixed traffic classes, goods locomotives, tank engines and the 'Standard' range designed for BR by Robert Riddles. Chapter 9 contains a main line stocklist which briefly details surviving main line locomotives and their locations at the time of going to press. Many of today's preserved locomotives can still be seen hard at work, pulling trains, but readers should remember that these engines require constant care and attention, and at intervals must be dismantled for inspection or repair — and in some cases this can take several years. Some locomotives pictured at work in this book may consequently be out-of-service for overhaul during your visit, whilst engines based at museums might have been withdrawn from display, possibly for a repaint — the National Railway Museum display also changes from time to time as the National Collection is too large to be displayed *en-masse*. Whilst this flexibility produces a dynamic and ever-changing vista, it can lead to disappointment if you are planning to travel a long distance to see or ride behind a particular locomotive. Please bear this in mind, and if possible, check in advance with the railway, steam centre or museum concerned.

CONTENTS

Chapter 1:
Essence of Steam **5**

Chapter 2:
Sheer Elegance **10**

Chapter 3:
Steam Supreme **27**

Chapter 4:
Zenith of Steam **46**

Chapter 5:
Mixed Traffic Locomotives **71**

Chapter 6:
Delivering the Goods **88**

Chapter 7:
Tank Engines **102**

Chapter 8:
The BR 'Standard' Locomotives **115**

Chapter 9:
Locomotive Stocklist **124**

Bibliography **128**

This edition of 'Steam All The Way has been produced exclusively for W.H. Smith & Son Ltd.

Published by: Silver Link Publishing Ltd., St Michael's on Wyre, Lancashire, England.

Copyright © Silver Link Publishing Ltd, 1987.
ISBN 0 947971 14 9.

Designed by Nigel Harris.
Typeset by Keystrokes, Morecambe.
Printed in Portugal by Printer Portuguesa

ACKNOWLEDGEMENTS

I would like to express my sincere thanks to all the photographers — too numerous to mention here individually — who have kindly made their work available for use in this book. Their help has been very much appreciated. Thanks are also due to John Coiley, John Bellwood, Bob Essery, Dick Riley, Keith Beck and Alan Middleton for their comments, help and advice regarding the text and captions — their specialist assistance was gratefully received and most useful. Finally, thanks to Peter Fox, of Platform 5 Publishing Ltd, for providing the information needed for Chapter 9. *Nigel Harris.*

FOREWORD
by
F.J. BELLWOOD
Chief Mechanical Engineer, National Railway Museum, York.

THE steam locomotive has an extraordinary fascination far beyond logical explanation, and whilst this is evident in many countries throughout the world, it is particularly so in Britain, where until relatively recently, the dream of almost every small boy was to eventually become an engine driver.

Perhaps National pride has something to do with it, for Britain did after all give the steam locomotive and railways to the world and by so doing provided mass land transport for all. This in turn enabled the dawning industrial revolution to rapidly advance, changing not only every aspect of manufacture but also the way of life of the population at large. But there must be more to it than that. Whilst to the lineside observer, a 'Pacific' in full cry at the head of an express passenger train is an impressive and awe-inspiring sight, the steam locomotive is in fact a noisy, smoky inefficient machine. To operate and maintain, it required hard, manual labour in anything but pleasant conditions. Yet the firemen who, in a typical day's work, had to shovel up to six tons of coal into the firebox, from an anything but stable 'platform', or fitters who struggled to change a heavy driving axlebox spring in an unheated, semi-open shed in the depths of winter, working in an inspection pit several inches deep in water, still speak with some affection of their time spent ministering to the needs of the steam locomotive. Whenever such men gather, conversation inevitably turns to the merits or otherwise of various locomotives, with the 'home product' being strongly defended if someone from another depot or Company has the temerity to voice a word of criticism! Surprisingly, after 20 years of experiencing the relative comforts of diesel and electric traction, this situation still applies, although few would wish to return to steam working days on a regular basis.

In the final analysis, it probably has as much to do with the human traits of the steam locomotive, as anything else. Temperamental, individualistic, responding on occasions to kindness and on others to harsh treatment, needing to be fed and watered in proportion to energy expanded, produced in all shapes and sizes but following a general form, requiring to be part of a team effort to give of its best, one could equally be referring to the steam locomotive or a human being.

The steam locomotive story can be told in many ways, invariably pertinent and interesting. Hundreds of books and articles have been written, but this is probably the first time an attempt has been made to do so using preserved examples to illustrate the development of the British steam locomotive. Such an approach is not without its difficulties, but it has the advantage that the reader can, by visiting the museums, steam centres and preserved railways referred to in the text, actually see and study the locomotives concerned. In fact, by becoming a member of the appropriate organisation, one can not only realise the childhood dream of becoming an engine driver, but also actively participate in the many other activities necessary to the running of a railway.

The problem with this approach is that not all significant advances in design are represented today, whilst other locomotives, of less importance to the development story are not only extant, but often duplicated. The survival after 1968 of a collection of engines in the hands of Dai Woodham, a South Wales scrap merchant, based at Barry Island, combined with the diverse needs, whims and fancies of the private preservation movement are largely responsible for the latter situation. When the Barry saga is long forgotten, future generations may well gain an entirely wrong impression about the importance of specific locomotive types, if judged solely by the number of such examples still in existence. The fact that only one solitary locomotive from the LNER, Britain's second largest railway, found its' way to Woodham's scrapyard amongst hundreds of others, illustrates the point.

Even the National Collection cannot be considered truly representative. The first Railway Museum in Britain was not opened in York until 1928, more than a century after *Locomotion* had triumphantly hauled the first train on the Stockton & Darlington Railway and not until as late as 1951 was a serious effort made to gather together and display a National Collection of Railway Relics. By this time, much had been lost forever, although there were fortunately some notable exceptions. Even then, only the main line system was considered and it was only after the opening of the National Railway Museum in 1975 that examples from the industrial railway scene were included. However, despite the shortcomings and obvious omissions, the National Collection does include some 80 steam locomotives dating from 1813 to 1960; the majority are unique and a significant proportion have been seen at work since the NRM opened in 1975 — exactly 150 years after the opening of the SDR.

Whilst it is the National Collection which should form the basis of any serious study of steam locomotive development in Britain, the private preservation movement has much to add, and in particular, offers the unique opportunity of experiencing at first-hand the merits and shortcomings of a variety of British locomotive designs, both from footplate and workshop viewpoints, as well as from the lineside and the train.

To those who believe that the steam locomotive died in Britain almost 20 years' ago, this book will at least cause surprise. Hopefully, it will do more than that and help foster a continued interest in Britain's greatest gift to the World — the steam locomotive.

F.J. Bellwood
Chief Mechanical Engineer,
National Railway Museum,
York.

CHAPTER 1:
ESSENCE
OF STEAM

Above: Bulleid 'West Country' class 'Pacific' No. 34092 *City of Wells*, normally resident on the Keighley & Worth Valley Railway, in West Yorkshire, leaves Hatton on November 2 1985 with 'The Shakespeare Limited' Sunday luncheon express from Marylebone, bound for Stratford upon Avon. *Mick Roberts.*

It is now nearly 20 years since the steam locomotive was banished from the national network of Great Britain, the country which had given the 'iron horse' to the world. After a century-and-a-half of faithful service, the fires were drawn for the last time in August 1968 at British Railways' final trio of run-down steam locomotive depots in North West England, at Carnforth, Lostock Hall (Preston) and Rose Grove (Burnley). Standard gauge BR steam passed into the history books and the everyday business of the railway was taken over by diesel and electric traction. Although these modern locomotives thereafter provided cleaner working conditions for their crews, and were in theory more efficient, they were characterless in comparison with the 'living' steam engines they replaced and for many people the thrill of standing at the lineside and watching a main line train pass disappeared. Yet in 1987 Britain is far from being starved of working steam engines — indeed, the country enjoys a variety and quality of steam locomotive operation for leisure purposes which is unmatched anywhere in the world. In the museums too, such as the superb National Railway Museum at York, or the GWR Museum at Swindon, there is a wealth of railway equipment, documents, uniforms and other artefacts displayed and interpreted with skill and care, for us to enjoy.

With steam gone from the main lines of Britain by the late summer of 1968, it was left to the working volunteers and financial supporters of the railway preservation movement to carry

THE
L. & H.R.
DECENNIUM
1973   1983

Left: The country's premier railway museum is the National Railway Museum, at York, which is based in a former steam locomotive shed. This view shows the main hall, with locomotives grouped around one of the two turntables. Note the 'smoke troughs' above the chimneys of the locomotives in the left background — these were used to carry smoke out of the building during its working days as an engine shed.
Joe Rajczonek.

working steam's torch forward into the last quarter of the 20th century. That they did not fail in their self-appointed task is clearly apparent, for in the summer months, or at Easter, Christmas, New Year, Bank Holidays and, at some locations, each weekend, steam locomotives of all shapes and sizes are at work around Britain. From tiny colliery shunter to main line giant, from humble coal wagon to opulent Pullman coach, the preservation movement has them all! To the continuing delight of generations of children who were never able to see steam locomotives in charge of the national system, the railway preservation movement has provided the opportunity, for both leiure and educational purposes, to take a step back into yesteryear.

Visit a private steam railway and you will find that in many cases the station staff wear immaculate vintage uniforms, complete with gleaming silver watch chains and polished buttons. On the neatly-swept platforms you will find milk churns, barrows carrying leather trunks and suitcases, whilst fences and walls will often be adorned with evocative enamel advertisements for products ranging from Stephens Inks to Ovaltine and Virol! Hanging baskets dripping with colour are delightful embellishments to the traditional station garden.

On a tranquil summer's day, or a crisp winter's morning, the scene is quite delightful and superbly evocative of the pre-Motorway age. Bells clang distantly in signal boxes, levers crash back and forth as the signalman sets the points, while wires squeak and rustle on their pulleys at the lineside as signals are cleared for the arrival of the train, which steams into the attractive scene to complete the tableau. It is an experience rich in atmosphere which should not be missed!

However, whilst museums and private railways provide much pleasure, they cannot provide the incomparable thrill of the main line express train rushing past, for under the strict Department of Transport regulations which govern their operations, trains are restricted to low speeds, normally 25mph. We have therefore been fortunate in recent years that the 'steam ban' imposed by BR over its main lines following the end of everyday steam operation in 1968 was lifted, after three years, in 1971. Since then, the appearance of a steam locomotive on a main line railtour has been certain to attract crowds in huge numbers to the fences, stations and bridges along its route. In the first half of the 1980s, paying passengers and trackside observers were given the opportunity to see a variety of painstakingly restored steam locomotives working hard over some of the country's most beautiful railway routes. These included the magnificent 'West Highland' extension' from Fort William to Mallaig in Western Scotland, and 'the road to the Isles' from Inverness to Kyle of Lochalsh.

Main line steam excursions also crossed the magnificent Forth Bridge, and Brunel's superb viaduct over the River Tamar at Saltash, in the West Country, whilst steam trains also delighted thousands of people by running on the scenic Settle-Carlisle line over the Pennines. Visitors and residents in the Welsh Marches were entertained by main line steam excursions, which were also popular between York, home of the National Railway Museum, and the seaside town of Scarborough. The celebration of the 150th anniversary of the Great Western Railway was held in 1985 and whilst this was marred by BR's announcement of the impending closure of Swindon Works, an extensive programme of main line steam trains in former GWR territory attracted

Facing Page: Small tank engines which once worked in private sidings across the country now play an important part on steam railways. On Cumbria's Lakeside & Haverthwaite Railway, 0-4-0ST *Caliban,* built at Bristol by the Peckett Company in 1937, awaits departure from Haverthwaite on June 5 1983, together with Hunslet 'Austerity' 0-6-0ST *Cumbria.*
Brian Dobbs.

STEAM-APPROVED BR ROUTES

MALLAIG 22
FORT WILLIAM
DUNDEE
PERTH
23
STIRLING
24
25 EDINBURGH
KILMARNOCK
AYR
26
NEWCASTLE
15
CARLISLE
MARYPORT
EAGLESCLIFFE
16
13
SCARBOROUGH
CARNFORTH
SETTLE
8
HARROGATE
12
YORK
10
11
9
HULL
14
LEEDS
MANCHESTER
5
4
SHEFFIELD
BUXTON
18
CHESTER
MATLOCK
NOTTINGHAM
PWLLHELI
19 DERBY
6
3
17
SHREWSBURY
MACHYNLLETH
ABERYSTWYTH
BIRMINGHAM
STRATFORD
CARMARTHEN
GLOUCESTER
1
27
SWANSEA
7
2
LONDON
DIDCOT
SWINDON
NEWPORT
21 ANDOVER
20
SALISBURY
YEOVIL

STEAM APPROVED BR ROUTES: MAP KEY

1: Marylebone — Stratford upon Avon — Tyseley
2: Didcot — Stratford upon Avon — Tyseley
3: Tyseley — Sheffield (via Derby or Toton)**
4: Sheffield — York
5: Sheffield — Manchester (via Hope Valley)
6: Manchester — Newport (via Chester & Shrewsbury)
7: Newport — Swindon (via Gloucester)
8: York — Scarborough
9: Hull — Selby — York — Leeds
10: Leeds — Harrogate — York
11: Leeds — Church Fenton — York
12: Leeds — Carnforth
13: Settle — Carlisle
14: Hellifield — Manchester Victoria (via Blackburn)
15: Carlisle — Newcastle — Eaglescliffe (via coast)
16: Carnforth — Maryport
17: Aberystwyth — Machynlleth — Pwllheli*
18: Derby — Buxton*
19: Nottingham — Matlock*
20: Salisbury — Yeovil*
21: Salisbury — Andover — Ludgershall*

22: Fort William — Mallaig
23: Edinburgh — Perth (via Stirling)
24: Edinburgh — Dundee (via bridges)***
25: Edinburgh suburban**
26: Carlisle — Kilmarnock — Ayr**
27: Swansea — Carmarthen*

Other steam routes not independently listed:
Nottingham — Marylebone** and Saltley — Sheffield**

*Reviewed annually;

**By special agreement

***Bridges barred, but open by special arrangement for Tay Bridge.

much attention. Steam returned in triumph in the 1980s to London, with the inauguration of an extremely successful programme of excursions from Marylebone to Stratford upon Avon, with passengers enjoying traditional Sunday lunches of roast beef as their train steamed north, towards the birthplace of Shakespeare. And these are just a few examples of the main line steam excursions which operated in the first half of the 1980s!

For today's youngsters, it is possibly the astronaut, or perhaps the pilot of the Harrier 'jump jet' or even *Concorde* who is the hero of the day, in command of the most up-to-date equipment that modern technology can provide. Possibly for our fathers, and almost certainly for our grandfathers, the driver of the express steam locomotive was the subject of this schoolboy admiration. He was regarded as a member of a respected social elite, not only by his fellow railwaymen, but also by working people from outside his industry. This was partly because railwaymen — and especially footplatemen — were regarded as having job security for life, but it was also inextricably linked with the mystique of the steam locomotive.

Of all mankind's many and wonderful inventions, the steam locomotive is probably unique in having been imbued with a life and personality of its own. From the smallest shunter to the crack express engine the steam locomotive is alive, powerful, full of character — and, above all, friendly. To young and old, and men and women alike, the steam locomotive has a directly emotional attachment which is perhaps difficult to articulate but impossible to deny. Little boys have stood on fences and gates for generations to wave to the cheerful figure of the engine driver in his cab, and this practice still survives wherever steam locomotives can be found at work. The friendly and charismatic appeal of the steam engine crosses all age groups, all professions, all sections of the population.

People *like* steam engines!

Railway photography has become increasingly popular as a hobby and many dedicated lensmen travel thousands of miles each year in pursuit of their quarry. Some of their subjects are static, and are pictured in their museum homes, but many more are working engines located in all parts of the country, in varied environments which present all kinds of challenges to those who seek to record their exploits on film. Few are professional photographers, but their work is second-to-none in terms of quality and this book is a tribute to their skills and endeavours. Within these pages you will find the steam locomotive in its many moods: aggressively at work, peacefully at rest, simmering in the night, providing a warm focus of attention on an icy winter day, or silhouetted against the setting sun. The steam locomotive is a marvellous subject for the photographer and there are many approaches to the subject from the traditional 'three-quarter' view of an approaching train, to a variety of more artistic interpretations. Many examples of these different styles are included in this book and they reflect great credit on the imagination and technique of the photographers concerned.

Steam All The Way is a tribute to all individuals and organisations which preserve and display historic railway artefacts of all kinds in the 1980s, but it is dedicated especially both to the unpaid volunteers of the railway preservation movement, and to those who have invested substantial sums of money in steam locomotives, frequently with little expectation of a return other than the pleasure they experience from seeing steam at work, and the pleasure it brings to others. These people in particular display a rare dedication, for there is far more to railways than the locomotives alone, and for every volunteer worker or fund-raiser devoted to the 'iron horse' itself there are more (frequently unsung) supporters whose interests and activities focus on vintage signalling equipment, antique wagons, the all-important trackwork, weeding the station gardens, issuing tickets, selling souvenirs and carrying out essential administration. *Steam All The Way* is dedicated to them all, with thanks. Please support their efforts, travel on their trains, perhaps even make a donation. Better still, join a preservation society and get involved yourself! It is still possible in this nuclear age to achieve the traditional schoolboy's dream of becoming an engine driver . . .

CHAPTER 2:
SHEER ELEGANCE

WITHIN Britain's population of around 55 million people it is estimated that there ae approximately two million railway enthusiasts. This interest embraces all walks of life, and of course the depth and extent of individual interest varies considerably. Some people are avid buyers of railway books and might pursue their interest from the armchair, whilst others are trainspotters, collecting locomotive numbers. Railway modelling in a variety of gauges and scales is also a popular pastime, whilst yet more people find enjoyment in their spare time as volunteer locomotive drivers, firemen, guards, signalmen, ticket clerks and fitters at the many steam centres and private railways which have become so common in the United Kingdom.

There are people who are interested in just about every aspect of railway history and operation, from the locomotives themselves down to buttons, badges and documents, but for many people it is the glamour, power, and sheer spectacle of the main line locomotive and train at speed which starts the adrenalin flowing. Whether or not you are interested in railways, it is undeniably impressive to stand at the lineside as a steam train approaches at speed, whistle screaming, before it roars past in a crescendo of sound, the carriage wheels beating a rhythmic tattoo on the track. There is perhaps a fleeting glimpse of smiling faces at windows and then the train is past, the rear of the last carriage fading rapidly into the distance as the billowing steam and smoke from the locomotive's chimney curls and dissipates in the air.

The steam locomotive at work is always an impressive blend of sound and vision, and while beauty is always in the eye of the beholder, few would deny that Britain's prestige main line steam locomotives have always been elegant and pleasing to the eye. This chapter of *Steam All The Way* provides a celebration of the magnificent main line engines we can still see, either in museums, or in steam and at work today, both on British Rail's main lines, and on privately operated steam railways. The choice is wide and the quality is superb — and when you consider that many of the working engines have been resurrected from scrapyard condition, largely at weekends, by volunteers financed in some cases only by a hard working souvenir sales department, their achievement becomes all the more impressive and admirable.

This country has a rich and varied selection of preserved steam locomotives which provide much enjoyment, including examples from all four private companies which operated the railways of Britain prior to Nationalisation in 1948 — the London Midland & Scottish Railway, the London & North Eastern Railway, the Great Western Railway and the Southern Railway. The old companies inspired great loyalty amongst their employees and supporters, together with rivalry of varying degrees of friendliness at all levels! This competitive spirit and fierce pride led to a variety of 'nicknames' for the railway companies. To the faithful disciples of Isambard Kingdom Brunel and his descendants, the GWR would always be 'God's Wonderful Railway', whilst others, mindful of the circuitous nature of the company's earlier main line routes, preferred the 'Great Way Round.'

At the time of its formation at the railway Grouping of 1923, the London Midland & Scottish Railway was the biggest joint-stock company operating a land-based transport system anywhere in the world. To many of its company servants, LMS stood for 'Lord's My Shepherd ', while others, less impressed, preferred 'Ell-of-a-mess' or 'Let Me Sleep'! The London & North Eastern Railway, which operated the East Coast Main Line from London King's Cross to Scotland, earned the reputation for being either the 'Late & Never Early Railway' or the 'London and Nearly Everywhere Railway!'

In serving their own parts of the country, each company developed its own locomotives, specifically suited to the tasks expected of them. Express passenger classes tended to be fitted with high-stepping large diameter driving wheels, which allowed high-speed running over long distances, whilst engines designed for goods traffic tended to have smaller wheels, enabling locomotives to develop the high power needed to pull heavy trains, but at the expense of high speed. Tank engines were also developed for different kinds of passenger and freight work, or perhaps a combination of both. Steam locomotives could have extremely long lives and the traditional practice was that as new and more powerful locomotives were introduced to tackle heavier, faster and longer distance trains, the engines they displaced were transferred to secondary and less exacting duties. In this way, some classes and types survived for many more years than might otherwise have been expected. Consequently, when it became clear to the railway enthusiasts of the country in the 1960s that steam traction was on its way into the history books, there were plenty of different locomotives available for preservation. A National Collection of locomotive types and classes judged to be especially important was assembled, though on a relatively low-key basis, and these engines, without any sort of official or permanent home, were stored at various locations around the country following withdrawal from service. Other engines in the care of the nation were displayed at the Museum of British Transport at Clapham, London, where locomotives like world speed record holder No. 4468 *Mallard* shared

During the 1960s, steam traction was swept from the national network at great speed, and working locomotives were scrapped long before the end of their useful lives. Left, above: On July 21 1960 GWR 'Castle' 4-6-0 No. 5043 *Earl of Mount Edgcumbe* passes Hanwell, West London, with an evening train from Paddington to Fishguard. This locomotive was withdrawn in December 1963 and despatched for scrap to Woodham's, of Barry, where No. 5043 is also pictured (Left, below) abandoned and forlorn, in 1968. The 4-6-0 was rescued in 1973 by the Birmingham Railway Museum, Tyseley.
Both: Mike Pope.

the hall with vintage trams and buses. Further historic engines were secure in the old York Railway Museum and other similar institutions. But the resources available to national bodies like British Railways for the preservation of important pieces of heritage were limited, and to the railway enthusiasts of this country it became very clear, very quickly, that these circumstances would inevitably and imminently result in the irretrievable loss of some very important locomotives.

Thus, the railway preservation movement was born as enthusiasts started buying engines, coaches, goods wagons and even entire sections of branch line. This principle had been established in 1950 with the preservation by enthusiasts of the 2ft 3in gauge Talyllyn Railway in North Wales, and as the 1950s drew to a close the Middleton Railway, in Leeds, and the Bluebell Railway, in Sussex, were cultivating the first seeds of standard gauge private railway preservation. The Middleton Railway, which used part of the trackbed of the first railway ever authorised by Act of Parliament, in 1758, reopened as a steam railway in June 1960 whilst the

Right, top: In 1968, more than 200 locomotives languished at Barry scrapyard, in South Wales, where they presented a sad sight. In October 1979, Riddles Class 2MT 2-6-0 No. 78059 and Bulleid 'Battle of Britain' Pacific No. 34073 *249 Squadron* (minus tender) awaited their fate. Locomotives rescued in similar dilapidated condition and since restored to running include No. 5690 *Leander* and No. 34092 *City of Wells,* both pictured elsewhere in these pages. *Tom Heavyside.*

Far right: Bulleid 'West Country' No. 34046 *Braunton* rusts in the salty air at Barry, in October 1979, a far cry from its days as a prestige express locomotive.

Near right: On the Mid Hants Railway, the fireman of 'West Country' No. 34016 *Bodmin* acknowledges the Guard's 'right-away' at Medstead & Four Marks, with a train for Alresford, on April 5 1986. *Bodmin* was rescued from Barry in 1972 and subsequently returned to steam in 1979.
Both: Tom Heavyside.

Bluebell Railway started running in August 1960.

In the early 1960s, the steam locomotive was being swept from the national network with ruthless speed before a relentless tide of modernisation, as rapidly increasing numbers of new diesel locomotives were introduced. Time was limited and many fine classes of locomotive went to the scrapyard before examples could be preserved. Nevertheless, many locomotives were successfully acquired for preservation, both from BR ownership until 1968, and subsequently from the South Wales scrapyard of Dai Woodham, at Barry. He bought hundreds of redundant locomotives from BR for scrap, but during the 1960s, 1970s, and even into the 1980s, his men were usually fully occupied cutting up scrap railway wagons, and the locomotives languished untouched on the dockside, slowly rusting away in the salty seaside air. A steady stream of preservationists rescued engines, some of which are now restored to immaculate running order and are illustrated in these pages, while others are still the subject of long-term repair. In 1968, 221 engines were packed into the sidings at Barry dock; by March 1987 only three dozen remained, awaiting their fate, 185 locomotives having been rescued by preservationists fully aware that maybe two decades of expensive, spare-time refurbishing and restoration work lay ahead. Of the rescued engines, 45 examples had been restored to working order by March 1987. The first locomotive to be rescued from Dai Woodham's yard, in 1968, was Midland Railway Fowler class 4F 0-6-0 No. 43924, which is still at work today on the Keighley & Worth Valley Railway, in Yorkshire. Other locomotives salvaged from the yard have included shunting engines, together with classes designed for the plodding haulage of lengthy, rumbling goods trains. However, the glamorous passenger engines lying in the wind-swept sidings attracted much attention and many have been brought back to life to join those locomotives officially or privately preserved in previous years. Examples include LMS 'Jubilee' 4-6-0 No. 5690 *Leander*, GWR 'Hall' 4-6-0 No. 6960 *Raveningham Hall*, Southern Railway 'West Country' 'Pacifics Nos. 34092 *City of Wells* and 34016 *Bodmin*, and, perhaps most spectacular of all, BR 4-6-2 No. 71000 *Duke of Gloucester*, which was in especially dilapidated and incomplete condition when it was bought by preservationists. Many people within even the steam world believed that it would be impossible to restore this engine to running order, but after 12 years of hard labour, both in raising finance and in the workshops, the 'Duke' did steam again, in 1986, as described in Chapter 8.

Amongst the restored ex-Barry engines working around the country today are the Brunswick green locomotives of the GWR, always a stirring sight with their polished copper-capped chimneys and gleaming brass name and numberplates. Complemented by their traditional 'chocolate and cream' carriages these engines are always a major attraction. The crimson locomotives and carriages of the LMS too provide a welcome splash of colour in the English landscape, whilst the bright malachite green or more demure olive green of the Southern Railway can also be seen in 1986. The apple green or garter blue of the LNER is also a familar sight to enthusiasts as a result of the many main line excursions undertaken in recent years by 'A3' 'Pacific' No. 4472 *Flying Scotsman* and 'A4' 'Pacific' No. 4498 *Sir Nigel Gresley*.

The express passenger locomotives at work in the 1980s vary greatly in age, but the survival of many important 'milestones' in locomotive development gives the keen observer the opportunity to trace the basic threads of the evolution of the express passenger engine. Some of the engines pictured in these pages still work regularly, some are steamed only rarely. Others have steamed for the last time and rest in honoured retirement, but whilst polished preservation on a museum plinth is perhaps less attractive to some observers than the locomotive at work, it is infinitely preferable to the locomotive as scrap.

As might be expected, the oldest surviving express passenger locomotives rarely survive in working order, but we are fortunate that some important early classes can still be seen in museums. The premier railway museum in the country is the National Railway Museum, in York, where many aspects of railway history are displayed. The Museum covers signalling, carriages, rolling stock and a host of other railway subjects, but locomotives feature prominently, and some fascinating early engines are featured.

George Stephenson and his immediate successors, pioneers as they were, shared various ideas which had a major influence on the design and appearance of their engines, including a belief that the locomotive's centre of gravity should be kept as low as possible (for safety reasons) and that the correct place for driving wheels was immediately beneath the boiler. The average speed of engines of the day was about 20mph, with a maximum, in very good conditions, of 40mph or

Left: **LMS 'Jubilee' No. 5690** *Leander* **follows the course of the River Severn, near Highley, on April 4 1986, with a Severn Valley Railway train, comprised principally of GWR rolling stock, en route from Bridgnorth to Kidderminster.**
John S. Whiteley.

Above: The oldest working steam locomotive in the world — Liverpool & Manchester Railway 0-4-2 *Lion*, built in 1838. This locomotive had a starring role in the Ealing comedy 'The Titfield Thunderbolt' and was restored to working order in time for the Rainhill celebrations of 1980, to mark the 150th anniversary of the LMR's opening. *Lion* is pictured here on September 6 1981, during a visit to the Worth Valley Railway. Note the large 'haycock' firebox, characteristic of the era. *Dave Dyson.*

Right: London & North Western Railway No. 2-2-2 *Cornwall*, owned by the National Railway Museum, seen during a period on loan to the Severn Valley Railway. The 1847-built locomotive is now based at the NRM. *Tim Grimshaw.*

so. Classic features of these early engines were the Gothic firebox, shielded in a polished brass casing, and minimal protection for the crew. The Furness Railways (later part of the LMS) 0-4-0 *Coppernob*, built by Edward Bury in 1846, was a comparatively late example illustrating some of these early principles.

Coppernob has a fascinating history: it worked for the FR until 1900 and after withdrawal was placed in an ornate glass display case outside Barrow-in-Furness station. There it remained until the Second World War, when a Luftwaffe bomb, probably intended for the town's famous shipyard, fell on the station, causing much damage and shattering *Coppernob's* cast-iron and glass shelter. Now displayed in the NRM, *Coppernob* still carries the shrapnel damage in its tender plates and boiler cladding sustained during the air raid.

Another interesting and particularly significant exhibit housed in the NRM is Grand Junction Railway 2-2-2 No. 1868 *Columbine*, only the 20th locomotive to be built at the Crewe 'engine manufactory', in 1845. A major problem for locomotive engineers of this era was that the wrought iron used to manufacture the crank axles of inside cylinder locomotives was unreliable and prone to failure. On the GJR, engineers Buddicom and Francis Trevithick responded by producing an outside cylinder locomotive of great strength and rigidity, of which *Columbine* was the first example. Known as the 'Crewe type', this design was used on the GJR, and subsequently on the London & North Western Railway, until 1857. Also part of the National Collection is LNWR 2-2-2 No.3020 *Cornwall*, a Crewe-type locomotive built at Crewe in 1847 and preserved in much rebuilt form.

The locomotive was still developing quickly at this stage and other factors played their part. Heavier train loads and the ever-present desire for higher speeds was a major spur, but there were also limitations, such as poor quality track, which had hindered advance. However, the introduction in 1862 of steel rails, together with the improvement of ballasting and better track drainage, paved the way for bigger, faster and more powerful locomotives.

The 2-4-0, a logical development of the 2-2-2, therefore became a popular express passenger type, and an attractive surviving example from the 1860s is Midland Railway 2-4-0 No. 158A, built at Derby in 1866. Not all locomotive engineers of these years were convinced by the potential of the 2-4-0, believing that the coupling of driving wheels would inhibit free running, compared with the 'single driver' types. On the MR however, Locomotive Superintendent Matthew Kirtley introduced this 2-4-0 class, known as the '156 class', in 1866. Fitted with distinctive double frames which partly covered the driving wheels, they were an immediate success on express services and although not the first 2-4-0s to be built by the MR, they were certainly one of the best-loved classes of the type built at Derby. They were small, but powerful, and 29 were built.

No. 158A had a particularly long life and after being renumbered on several occasions it was finally withdrawn from service in 1947. The LMS appreciated the historical importance of the engine, which was restored in MR livery as No. 158A, in which form it is preserved today at the Midland Railway Centre, Butterley, near Derby. The splendid crimson livery is indeed evocative

Right: LNWR 2-4-0 No. *Hardwicke* at work giving brake van rides on the short demonstration line at the Dinting Railway Centre, near Manchester, on May 2 1982. A distinguished member of the National Collection, *Hardwicke* is now resident at the National Railway Museum. *Alan Tyson.*

Below: Sheer elegance — Patrick Stirling's GNR 4-2-2 No. 1 passes Woodthorpe, on the Great Central Railway, with a four-coach passenger train on Saturday June 12 1982, following its restoration to working order at the NRM, in 1981. Prior to this, No. 1 had last worked in 1938. *Graham Wignall.*

of what has come to be regarded as the 'Midland tradition' — but it is interesting to note that crimson lake was introduced to the MR only in 1883. Prior to this date all Midland engines had been green.

Other 2-4-0s surviving on museum display in the 1980s include North Eastern Railway No. 2-4-0 No. 910 (built 1875) and LNWR 'Precedent' class No. 790 *Hardwicke*, built at Crewe in 1892, both at the NRM. *Hardwicke* especially illustrates the longevity of the 2-4-0 type and during the 'Races to the North' of 1895, when the 4-4-2 and the 4-6-0 types were being developed, the locomotive established a speed record between Crewe and Carlisle which remained unchallenged until 1936!

One of the oldest 'top link' locomotives to survive in working order in the 1980s is Patrick Stirling's 4-2-2 No. 1, built for the Great Northern Railway in 1870 for use on prestige Anglo-Scottish trains on the East Coast Main Line from King's Cross. The locomotive and its 53 sisters were fitted with huge single pairs of 8ft diameter driving wheels, leading to their becoming universally known as 'Stirling Singles.' No. 1 is extremely elegant in appearance and is typical of the single driving wheel locomotive type which came back into vogue in the late 19th century, following the invention of steam powered sanding equipment, which placed sand on the rails in front of the driving wheels, giving the valuable advantage of increased 'grip' on wet or greasy rails. This enabled the engines to successfully handle their trains, at this time still comprised of relatively light vehicles of four and six-wheeled design. The 'Stirling Singles' were fine express engines, and they performed well on the uphill stretches of the GNR main line, where sustained steaming and power output were required. On the downhill sections of track their large wheels enabled them to run swiftly and impressively.

Stirling's 4-2-2s handled principal GNR expresses in the last quarter of the 19th century and created a mystique surrounding East Coast express power which was later inherited and taken to new heights by Gresley's magnificent 'Pacifics.' The 'Singles' also played a key part in the famous 'Races to the North' of 1888 and 1895, when vigorous competition broke out between East and West Coast routes for the Anglo-Scottish traffic. In 1888 the competition focussed on the London-Edinburgh trains, following a decision by the GNR in November 1887 to allow third class passengers to travel on the 10 o'clock morning train from King's Cross to Edinburgh Waverley, with a booked journey time of nine hours. The West Coast route, operated from

Above: A pleasing portrait of the 'Stirling Single' in the shed yard at Loughborough, on the great Central Railway. The driving wheels are 8ft in diameter.
Graham Wignall.

London Euston by the London & North Western Railway, also made provision for third class passengers on its best comparable services — but with a longer journey time of up to 10 hours. After some consideration, the LNWR (in conjunction with the Caledonian Railway, with which it jointly operated the West Coast route) cut its London-Edinburgh journey time to 9 hrs in June 1888. The East Coast route partners replied with an even more competitive 8½-hr service, prompting in response a matching journey time by the West Coast route. As a consequence, the GNR announced an even faster 8-hr schedule, and eventually both companies were running theoretically on a 7¾-hour schedule, but the contest ended after the East Coast route achieved a timing of 7 hrs 32 min for the 392.8 mile run — six minutes better than the West Coast route's timing.

In 1895 the 'racing' started again, following the opening of the Forth Bridge, which gave the East Coast route a 15-minute advantage over its West Coast competitors for the night services to Aberdeen. Thus, on June 1 1895 the West Coast route cut 10 minutes from the timing of its 10'o clock departure from Euston, giving its service an arrival time at Aberdeen within five minutes of that of the East Coast train from King's Cross. Sharp competition was in the air once again: timetables were ignored, common sense was apparently forgotten and the operation evolved quickly into a hammer-and-tongs dash for the finishing line with a few token coaches coupled to the locomotive tenders. Enginemen and locomotives both showed their qualities to great effect, but, in the final instance, it was the signalman at Kinnaber Junction who really decided each night which train rolled into its destination first, for from his outpost both East and West Coast trains shared the Caledonian Railway tracks to Aberdeen.

On August 22 1895, the West Coast train arrived at Aberdeen from Euston, a distance of 540 miles, in 512 minutes, an average speed overall of 63.3mph. This might seem a quite ordinary speed by today's standards, but at the time it was utterly spectacular, and included a run between Crewe and Carlisle — which included the gruelling climbs over Grayrigg summit and Shap Fell, in Westmorland — at an average speed of 57mph. The locomotive in charge was LNWR 'Precedent' 2-4-0 *Hardwicke*, and this record remained unbroken until November 1936, when Stanier 'Pacific' No. 6201 *Princess Elizabeth* set a new standard, as described in Chapter 4. *Hardwicke* survives today as part of the National Collection, and we can only wonder at what the conditions must have been like in the sparsely protected cab that night in the Westmorland Fells, and admire the enginemen for their skill and determination. Quite what sort of quality of ride the passengers experienced as their train was whisked northwards on that epic journey is another matter entirely!

The resurgence of the single driving wheel type in the late 19th century was rather unrepresentative, for the 4-4-0 had been developing as an express passenger locomotive since about 1870, and by the mid-1890s was handling most fast trains. Whilst the single driving wheel type did much useful work in these years it would be wrong to overestimate their importance, for less than 250 were built — less than five per cent of the top flight passenger power of the era. GNR No. 1 was the first of the class of 53 engines, and was built at Doncaster, where it was based for its entire working life of 37 years. It was preserved following withdrawal in 1907, when it was envisaged that the locomotive would spend its retirement as a museum piece. However, in 1938 the locomotive was restored to working order as part of the LNER's promotional activities in connection with the introduction of new rolling stock for its famous 'Flying Scotsman' train, which ran non-stop between King's Cross and Edinburgh. The Victorian locomotive ran on several excursions at this time and appeared alongside Gresley's streamlined 'A4' class 'Pacifics', with which it provided a strong contrast.

Having experienced its brief moment of glory in 1938, No. 1's GNR green livery was groomed to immaculate perfection and the locomotive was placed on display in the York Railway Museum, where it remained until the establishment of the National Railway Museum, also in York, in 1975. The historic locomotive received an honoured place in the splendid new Museum, where it continued to delight and enthral visitors. Once again, and not unreasonably, it was assumed that the 105-years old veteran was finally retired — but this was not the case. In late 1981, GNR No. 1 was restored at the NRM and transferred by road to the Great Central Railway, where on December 2 the locomotive was steamed in public for the first time since 1938, under the guidance of NRM Chief Mechanical Engineer John Bellwood. The boiler pressure was reduced from 170 pounds per square inch (psi) to 110 psi, but this was sufficient for the grand old lady to haul short trains at a sedate pace on the GCR's five-mile line from Loughborough to Rothley.

No. 1 'played to packed houses' over several weekends in service on the GCR before returning to its home at the NRM. Since then the 'Single' has briefly visited the North Yorkshire Moors Railway, where it was steamed for filming work for the BBC. Under normal circumstances No. 1 is displayed with pride in the main hall of the NRM, where it stands as an evocative reminder of a pioneering era in the history of railways, when the express steam locomotive was the wonder of the age and man had yet to fly.

A further particularly attractive preserved example of the single driving wheel type is Caledonian Railway 4-2-2 No. 123, built in 1886 by the Neilson company, for display at the International Exhibition of Industry, Science & Art, held in Edinburgh that year. Following closure of the exhibition the 4-2-2 was taken into CR stock as No. 123. In 1884, two years previously, the 'Caley's' CME, Dugald Drummond, had introduced a powerful new class of 4-4-0,

Left: Above: GWR 4-4-0 No. 3440 *City of Truro* is paired with Caledonian Railway 4-2-2 No. 123 at Old Oak Common, London, in 1960. No. 123 is preserved today as a non-working exhibit of the Glasgow Museum of Transport.
R.C. Riley.

Left, below: MR 4-2-2 No. 673, known as 'The Spinner', on display in the locomotive yard at Butterley, at the Midland Railway Centre. This locomotive is now based at the National Railway Museum.
Tom Heavyside.

a much more modern and powerful type which had effectively superseded the 'Single', and it is therefore surprising that No. 123 was built at all. In 1888 however, No. 123 proved its mettle, working between Carlisle and Edinburgh, over the notorious climb to Beattock, during the 'Races to the North' of that year. Her best trip resulted in an average speed of 60mph, despite stiff climbs to both Beattock and Cobbinshaw, north of Carstairs. In LMS days, No. 123 went back into ordinary service, primarily on local services on the Perth-Dundee line, where the engine became the last 'Single' in Britain to remain in revenue-earning service. As LMS No. 14010 the engine was withdrawn in 1935, preserved and repainted in CR blue livery and stored at St Rollox works. In 1958 No. 123 was recommissioned and spent several years in railtour service, finally being moved to the Glasgow Museum of Transport in 1965. The locomotive was taken off public view in 1987 following closure of the original museum, in Albert Drive, during preparations for the move to a new home at the Kelvin Hall, Argyll Street, Glasgow.

As on the GNR, the 'Single' also returned in the last decade of the 19th century on the express passenger services of the Midland Railway, and 4-2-2 No. 673 was built in 1897 at Derby as one of 95 locomotives completed between 1887 and 1900. This extremely elegant locomotive was withdrawn from traffic in 1928 and subsequently preserved by the LMS. The 'Spinner', as No. 673 is generally known, was restored to working order at the Midland Railway Centre, Butterley, in time for the Rainhill celebrations of 1980, held to commemorate the 150th anniversary of the opening of the Liverpool & Manchester Railway in 1830. No. 673 painted in the MR crimson lake livery of the post-1907 period, is normally displayed at the NRM.

Following the 'Races to the North' of 1895, the East and West Coast companies agreed that their premier London − Glasgow/Edinburgh trains should not reach their destinations in less than eight hours. This certainly put a stop to the dangerous 'racing' − especially after a disastrous accident involving a northbound express at Preston in August 1896 − but it also hampered the natural development of Anglo-Scottish services for the next 30 years. However, this agreement could not halt development of the locomotive itself, and the 1890s saw the end of

Above: Whilst most British companies favoured 4ft 8½in as the distance between the rails, the GWR believed that a wider gauge of 7ft ¼in would give greater stability and enable higher speed running. However, the 4ft 8½in distance was adopted as a standard gauge throughout the country and in 1892 the broad gauge was finally abolished. No original main line broad gauge engines survive today, but this splendid working reproduction of *The Iron Duke* was built for the Science Museum by Resco (Railways) Ltd. in 1985. It is seen here running on temporary track in Kensington Gardens, in April 1985. *The Iron Duke* is based at the National Railway Museum. *Peter Zabek.*

Right: This non-working reproduction of GWR Dean Bogie 'Single' standard gauge 4-2-2 No. 3041 *The Queen* was built in 1982 by Steamtown, Carnforth, for Madame Tussaud's Victorian 'Royalty and Empire' exhibition constructed at Windsor station. *John Shuttleworth.*

the 'Single's' resurgence as front line passenger power. Locomotives fitted with four-coupled driving wheels thereafter held sway.

In 1900, about 20,000 locomotives were at work on Britain's railways, of which fully half were engines of the 0-6-0 and 4-4-0 wheel arrangements. The 4-4-0 was the classic and most widespread British passenger engine of the time, and by 1914 almost every English and Scottish railway company had built engines of this wheel arrangement. Exceptions included the Maryport & Carlisle Railway, on the Western fringes of the English Lake District, and the coal-carrying companies of the South Wales valleys, which had no use for such passenger locomotives. By the time of the railway Grouping of 1923, the 4-4-0 was by far the most numerous type of passenger engine in the land, and every last one of the 20 major constituent companies of the 'Big Four' railways contributed one or more classes of 4-4-0. For example, the LMS inherited nearly 1,100 engines of this type, with more than 400 coming from the former Scottish companies, and more than 350 from the MR alone.

The British 4-4-0 started developing in earnest in the 1870s, during which decade the steam locomotive assumed a basic appearance which it retained until the end of steam construction by British Railways in 1960, with the emergence of Riddles 9F 2-10-0 No. 92220 *Evening Star* from Swindon Works. Although 4-4-0s had existed before the 1870s, they had been imperfect and consequently unpopular, and whilst the first successful example of the type had been North British Railway 4-4-0 No. 224 (the locomotive fated to fall into the Firth of Tay in the infamous Tay Bridge disaster of Sunday December 28 1879) the 4-4-0 can be better traced to the Great Eastern and Midland Railway types of the middle 1870s. Nevertheless, in this decade the 4-4-0 still had a spirited rival in the less expensive 2-4-0, and engines of this latter type remained in favour on the MR and the NER for express passenger work. Some 2-4-0s survived, albeit in small numbers, beyond the Grouping of 1923.

From the 1870s, 4-4-0s tended to have cylinders and valve gear mounted between the main frames, though examples with outside cylinders continued to appear. Development of the 4-4-0 continued through the second half of the 19th century and many would claim that its finest hour came with the magnificent 'Dunalastair' 4-4-0s of the Caledonian Railway. These locomotives were introduced in the aftermath of the 1895 races for Aberdeen, and their performances on fast, non-stop trains running over long distances were quite fantastic for their day. Unfortunately,

Below: William Stroudley's 0-4-2 No. 214 *Gladstone* was built in 1882 for express passenger duties on the London Brighton & South Coast Railway. Although this class was very successful, the 0-4-2 type was not generally regarded as being suitable for high speed work. Upon withdrawal in 1927 *Gladstone* was purchased by the Stephenson Locomotive Society as Britain's first privately preserved standard gauge locomotive, and presented to the York Railway Museum. Now part of the National Collection, *Gladstone* is pictured here at Sheffield Park, Bluebell Railway, on July 18 in its centenary year of 1982. This locomotive is now based at York. *Peter Zabek.*

none of these locomotives survived into preservation, but we are lucky to have several other examples of this interesting and important type of locomotive in the preserved fleet. Some of these 4-4-0s are preserved in non-working order in our railway museums, such as the NRM's NER class 'M' No. 1621, built in 1893 for express service and designed by Wilson Worsdell. No. 1621, one of a class of 20 engines, displayed its soundness of design on the night of August 21/22 1895, when it averaged 61.5mph for the 124 ¾ miles between Newcastle and Edinburgh. The engine was withdrawn from service by the LNER from Alnmouth shed in July 1945, and preserved in view of its prestigious past. No. 1621 was re-painted in gleaming NER green livery in 1975, by the British Rail Engineering Ltd Carriage Works, in York. Other classic British inside-cylindered 4-4-0s on museum display today include Great North of Scotland Railway No. 49 *Gordon Highlander* (built 1920) and North British Railway No. 256 *Glen Douglas* (built 1913), in the care of the Glasgow Museum of Transport.

Right: North Eastern Railway 'M' class 4-4-0 No. 1621, standing outside the NRM, York. This locomotive recorded some very high speed running during the 'Races to the North' between London and Aberdeen, in 1895. *John Coiley.*

One of the oldest examples of an inside-cylinder 4-4-0 maintained in working order is Drummond 'T9' 4-4-0 No. 30120, now preserved as a member of the National Collection, but based on the Mid Hants Railway, in Hampshire. Designed by Dugald Drummond and known as 'Greyhounds' for their sleek lines and speedy qualities, the 'T9' 4-4-0s were introduced in 1899 and by 1901 66 examples had been constructed for the London & South Western Railway. A second batch of 20 engines followed and the 'T9s' were the cornerstone of South Western passenger traffic at least until the Grouping of 1923. In the first years of the 20th century, the 'Greyhounds' were in the front-line of the LSWR's vigorous competition with the GWR for the West of England passenger traffic, which was not only profitable, but highly prestigious. They became particularly well-known for their sparkling performances on expresses to Exeter. During the struggles of World War 1 the class bore the brunt of many passenger services whilst the LSWR's larger 4-6-0s were otherwise engaged on trains directly concerned with the war effort — troop, ambulance, explosives and heavy goods workings. The 'Greyhounds' had a long and useful life and were still to be seen on secondary duties for BR's Southern Region in 1961, when they were more than 60 years old!

Whilst still in BR stock, No. 30120 was overhauled at Eastleigh Works, from where it emerged respendent in LSWR green livery in March 1962, for use on railtour workings. Final withdrawal from service came in July 1963 and as LSWR No. 120 the locomotive finally passed into retirement after a working life of nearly 64 years. The engine spent some time at the Birmingham Railway Museum, Tyseley, before being put into store in the reserve collection at the National Railway Museum, York, where it was not on public display. In 1981, the NRM loaned the 'T9' to the MHR, where it has since been restored to working order. To the disappointment of some enthusiasts, but the delight of others, the engine has been painted not in LSWR green, but in lined BR black livery as No. 30120, in which form it ended its normal working life for the national network. The 'T9' can thus be seen earning its keep on the MHR's line between Alresford and Alton, where steam trains connect with BR's electric services. The MHR has done a superb job of restoring the 'T9', giving everyone an opportunity to see a classic British locomotive of pre-World War 1 days in steam and hauling passenger trains. It reflects great credit not only on the volunteers and full-time staff of the' Watercress Line', but also on the officers of the National Railway Museum, York. Without their understanding and co-operation such marvellous sights would not be possible and their foresight deserves appreciation.

In its simplest form, a steam locomotive works by boiling water to make steam, which is then passed, via a regulator valve, to the cylinders, where it is used, either in volume or expansively, to move the pistons, which through connecting rods and coupling rods, turn the wheels to move the engine along the rails. Once the piston has moved through its stroke, the steam is exhausted to the atmosphere, through the chimney, with a loud 'chuff'. This is a 'simple' steam engine. However, after the steam has been used in one cylinder, it can be used again at least once or

twice, at a lower pressure in secondary cylinders, before being exhausted to the atmosphere. Described as 'compound' working, this makes more economical use of the coal and water, but the design has its own problems when applied to railway locomotives, including increased maintenance costs, and compounding never really 'caught on' widely in this country. The LNWR experimented with various types of comound engines, with varying degrees of success, but most other companies preferred simple designs.

The Midland Railway was unique amongst British railway companies in developing a compound locomotive as its premier express class. In 1902, MR Locomotive Superintendent S. W. Johnson introduced his pioneer compound locomotive, which as No. 1000 survives today as a member of the National Collection. That the class was built in successive batches for the next 30 years is ample testimony to the success of the design. A total of 45 examples were built at Derby before the Grouping, with a further 195 being constructed after 1923, though modifications were incorporated by the LMS, including adaptation from right to left-hand drive, and the addition of steam superheating. The LMS-built engines also differed in being fitted with 6ft 9in diameter driving wheels, in place of the 7ft wheels provided on the original MR engines. Throughout the 1920s and early 1930s, the compound 4-4-0s regularly hauled express passenger trains, until the arrival of larger locomotives designed by William Stanier. Thereafter, the class worked in a more secondary capacity, their numbers eventually dwindling through the 1950s until, by 1961, only two examples of the class of 239 engines survived. No. 41168 was the final survivor, being condemned in July 1961.

The preserved 'Compound,' originally numbered 2631 and rather different in appearance to how it looks today, was renumbered 1000 in the MR renumbering scheme of 1907; it was withdrawn as BR No. 41000 in October 1951 after which it languished in the Crewe Works paintshop. In June 1959 it was reinstated for working special trains and was painted in 1907 MR crimson lake livery before returning to work. It was subsequently displayed at the Museum of British Transport, Clapham, before being transferred to the NRM in time for its opening in 1975. The locomotive has been maintained in working order, working a variety of main line special trains, to wide public acclaim.

Above: Hampshire's Mid Hants Railway, known as the 'Watercress Line', boasts an impressive stud of working main line locomotives, including the National Railway Museum's Drummond class 'T9' 4-4-0 No. 30120. This locomotive is seen here climbing away from the MHR's southern terminus, at Alresford, with a passenger train for Ropley. *Mike Esau.*

Right: Pioneer MR 'Compound' 4-4-0 No. 2631, in original 1902 condition — although the locomotive is fitted with temporary 'shelters' flanking the smokebox, used to accommodate engineers during scientific testing. *Bob Essery Collection.*

Above: No. 2631 was re-numbered 1000 in 1907, and this historic locomotive survives today as illustrated here, as a member of the National Collection, based at the NRM, York. *John Coiley.*

As the end of the 19th century approached, the railway companies of Great Britain were under increasing pressure to provide heavier and faster trains. Until then, passenger stock had consisted of short vehicles of four and six-wheeled construction, with individual compartments and no side corridors or inter-connecting gangways between vehicles. Trains were short and relatively light, so the modest 2-2-2s, 4-2-2s and 4-4-0s had mastered them with comparative ease. On longer journeys, such as those linking London with Scotland, locomotives had been changed at regular intervals, much as horses had been changed on the long coaching routes of the previous age. These stops were also utilised to enable passengers to take refreshment, and no doubt other much-needed breaks — remember, in the carriages of this era, once the train started you were trapped in your compartment until the next stop!

Trains such as the 'Flying Scotsman' en-route between King's Cross and Edinburgh, or the LNWR Anglo-Scottish express, mid-way between Glasgow and Euston, called at York and Preston respectively for around 20 minutes to allow passengers a hasty lunch. Restaurant cars of Pullman design had been introduced into Britain as early as 1879 by the Great Northern Railway, and in the subsequent decade others were provided on long distance trains, especially those running north from London. However, apart from Pullman cars, no corridor stock existed to allow movement through the train: passengers wishing to eat on board had to join the dining car at a station, and remain in it until the next stop. Thus, as late as 1900, 21 years after the GNR had

introduced its first dining car, the prestigious 'Flying Scotsman' was still pausing for 20 minutes at York.

The first true corridor train had arrived on British metals in 1892, with the introduction by the GWR of gangwayed stock, with end connections. What have since come to be regarded as conventional compartments were featured in these new coaches, with a side corridor; dining cars were of an open design with a central walkway, flanked by tables and chairs. Corridor stock was progressively introduced around the country thereafter and new coaches put into service on the East Coast Main Line in 1900 finally enabled the 'Flying Scotsman' to abandon its traditional layover at York.

As carriages grew in size to be carried on bogies, and trains grew in length to become increasingly heavy, the inadequacies of the comparatively lightweight motive power were brought into sharp focus, for a heavy train needed a powerful locomotive to haul it. Furthermore, once the driver started his train and it gained speed and momentum, he needed an efficient and powerful brake with which to bring it safely to a stand. The Regulation of Railways Act of 1889 had stipulated that all passenger trains should have continuous brakes, whereby brake shoes could be applied to each wheel of the train to give the driver complete and confident control. The brakes were operated on a fail-safe system, with the brakes being kept 'off' by either a

Above: GNR 'Atlantic' No. 990 *Henry Oakley*, **outside the NRM, York. The 4-4-2 wheel arangement, new to this country in 1898, was already common in America and thus became known in Britain as the 'Atlantic'.** *John Coiley.*

Below: Ivatt's larger development of the 'Atlantic' type is represented today in the National Collection by No. 251, built in 1902 and pictured here on display at a BR open day at Doncaster Works, on July 28 1984. *Dave Dyson.*

vacuum or a degree of air pressure in the control pipe, which stretched the length of the train. If the train divided for any reason, the brakes would be fully and immediately applied, bringing both portions to a standstill and minimising the risk of accident or injury.

In the early years of the 20th century, the passenger carriage developed as a vehicle of great opulence, growing quickly to the maximum size permitted by the limitations of the British loading gauge — 13 ft high, approximately 9ft wide and between 50ft and 70ft in length. Locomotives of greater capacity and speed were needed and the designers produced the 'Atlantic' 4-4-2 wheel arrangement, a significant link in the chain of express British locomotive types between the single driving wheel design, such as GNR No. 1, and the 'Pacific' 4-6-2s, as represented in preservation by locomotives like *Flying Scotsman* and *Duchess of Hamilton*. The 4-4-2, new to this country at the end of the last century, was named 'Atlantic' as the type had been in use in America for several years. The first example was Ivatt's No. 990 *Henry Oakley*, built for the GNR in 1898 and now preserved at the National Railway Museum. The locomotive was named after the Company's General Manager — only the second GNR locomotive to carry a name. The 4-4-2 wheel arrangement enabled the provision of a much longer boiler and wider firebox than had been possible previously, and Ivatt's first 'Atlantics' represented a significant step forward in power and speed on the East Coast Main Line.

Experience gained with No. 990 led Ivatt to further develop the potential of the 'Atlantic' wheel arrangement and in 1902, the larger-boilered GNR 4-4-2 No. 251 appeared, an improved design which made the most of the possibilities offered by the type. A total of 21 of the original 1898 design were built, followed by 91 examples of the larger 1902 version, whose generously proportioned boiler and firegrate ensured a plentiful supply of steam. This enabled the large 'Atlantics' to be worked extremely hard for long periods and these strengths were used to the full in the dark days of the First World War, when the Ivatt 'Atlantics' performed much valuable service on the East Coast Main Line. They handled all principal GNR main line trains until 1922, when Gresley's first 'Pacifics' were introduced, shortly before the Grouping which amalgamated the GNR into the LNER. After 30 years at work the Ivatt 'Atlantics' were modified with large capacity steam superheating equipment and as a result they were rejuvenated as express locomotives, being capable of deputising for Gresley's much larger 'Pacifics', when required, on exacting prestige duties. The pioneer engine of the class, No. 251, has an eminent place in the National Railway Museum, at York.

The 'Atlantic' was a locomotive of beauty and elegance which easily assumed the charismatic mantle created by the 'Stirling Singles', and the Ivatt engines enjoyed a popular public profile. However, their period of pre-eminence was relatively brief, for No. 251 was still brand new when the 4-6-0 type, especially as designed by Chief Mechanical Engineer George Jackson Churchward on the GWR, was showing superior capabilities of power and endurance. Consequently, the 'Atlantic' was short-lived in most respects: all 309 examples of the type were built over a 22 year span, and this total represented no more than 16 per cent of the top flight express motive power fleet of the time. Although important they were quickly superseded and we are therefore fortunate that pioneers No. 990 and 251 survive for us to enjoy today.

The locomotive engineers of the last decade of the 19th century had been conservative in outlook, and it was only the increasing requirement to work heavier and faster trains as the 1890s progressed that prompted the introduction of bigger locomotives by the turn of the century. Even so, the locomotives concerned were only an improvement on the preceeding 2-4-0s and 4-4-0s inasmuch as they were bigger and heavier: they were simply larger examples of existing practice and they did not represent any significant advance in steam generation and usage. The locomotives of this era represented the end of this particular phase of steam locomotive development and it was left to George Jackson Churchward, the perceptive Chief Mechanical Engineer of the Great Western Railway, to write the next chapter of steam locomotive design.

CHAPTER 3:
STEAM SUPREME

In the 20th century, the 4-6-0 and 4-6-2 ('Pacific') wheel arrangements became the two most popular forms of motive power in Great Britain for long distance haulage of semi-fast and express passenger trains. Of the 'Big Four' private railway companies which existed until Nationalisation on January 1 1948, the GWR was unique in never employing anything larger than a 4-6-0 on a regular basis, even for its prestige expresses. On the other hand, the LMS under William Stanier, the LNER under Nigel Gresley (both designers subsequently being knighted) and the SR under Oliver Bulleid, all introduced impressive 'Pacifics' for their heaviest and fastest passenger workings.

This is something of a paradox, for GWR Chief Mechanical Engineer George Jackson Churchward had designed and built Britain's first engine of the 4-6-2 wheel arrangement, his ungainly *The Great Bear* of 1908. However, the extreme length and weight of this engine (for the time) limited its use primarily to the London-Bristol main line and while Churchward was said to be fond of his massive creation, it was not regarded as a successful design and no more were built. It has even been argued that the GWR Board of Directors ordered its construction more for the publicity it would create for the Company, rather than its operational use. *The Great Bear* certainly cannot be regarded as being in the mainstream of GWR development, other than as an exercise in large boiler construction.

In the years before 1910 Churchward is best remembered for his development of the 4-6-0,

Above: Was this the first locomotive to achieve 100mph? In 1904 GWR 4-4-0 No. 3440 *City of Truro* is reputed to have reached just over 102mph during a run from Plymouth to Bristol, but this has been the subject of much controversy ever since. Restored to working order in 1985, No. 3440 is seen here passing Safari Park, on the Severn Valley Railway, in charge of the 11.50 am departure from Bridgnorth, of April 1 1986. *Andrew Bell.*

which in both four and two-cylinder forms provided the basis for Swindon-built motive power virtually to the end of steam construction and operation on British main lines. The principles which Churchward established at this time are all clearly evident on the preserved engines of the GWR which can still be seen either in museums, or running on private railways, in the 1980s. Even to the untrained eye, the preserved locomotives of the GWR all have a strong family resemblance, and this stemmed from the standardisation programme inaugurated by Churchward in the early years of this century. To place the preserved 'Castles', 'Kings', 'Halls' and 'Manors' in their true perspective, and to see how Churchward's work influenced locomotive development generally in the 20th century, it is of interest to briefly examine his approach from 1902. Churchward's work was far in advance of his contemporaries, especially in boiler design, enabling the GWR to produce its ultimate locomotive, the 'King' class 4-6-0, in 1927.

Churchward's influence in GWR motive power matters had been steadily increasing during the final years of William Dean's tenure as Chief Mechanical Engineer, and when Churchward succeeded as CME in 1902 he was ideally placed to start work immediately on the development of his own ideas. Thus, his first 4-6-0 appeared in February 1902 (covered in more detail later in this chapter) and in September 1902, 'Atbara' class 4-4-0 No. 3405 *Mauritius,* then barely a year old, was taken into Swindon works and fitted with a Churchward standard No. 4 taper boiler. The modified design was immediately successful for in 1903, ten new locomotives of the revised design were built, and between 1907 and 1909 a further nine 'Atbaras' were modified to join the class, which were all named after famous English cities. One of the 1903 engines, No. 3440 *City of Truro,* still with us today as part of the National Collection, earned its place in the history books in May 1904, when it was claimed to have achieved a maximum speed of 102.3mph during a whirlwind descent of Wellington Bank, in Somerset — the first steam locomotive in the world to reach 100mph.

This claim has fuelled much debate amongst railway enthusiasts ever since, for whilst a high-speed run into the '90s' is not disputed, quite whether the 4-4-0 actually broke into 'three figures' is a matter of some doubt. The 'City' class locomotives were in many ways outmoded engines even at the time of their construction: for example, they featured double frames, which were very much a hallmark of the 19th century and were relatively small engines at a time when the general trend was towards larger designs. Even measured against contemporary 4-4-0s from other companies, they were lightweight in appearance and performance. Neverthless, the class had well-designed valves and cylinders which made the best use of the superb boiler's output, to create a fast, free-running locomotive which the GWR put to good use on its 'Ocean Mails' expresses,linking Plymouth with London.

At this time, powered flight was in its infancy and all long-haul land travel was by rail, with inter-continental travel only by mighty ocean liner. Trans-Atlantic ships docking at Plymouth brought cargoes of passengers and mails from the United States of America, and the London & South Western Railway and the GWR companies competed vigorously for the fastest link from the dockside to London. These were the circumstances in which No. 3440 *City of Truro* made its reputed record run.

On May 9 1904, the Norddeutscher Lloyd liner *Kronprinz Wilhelm* arrived in Plymouth with a cargo of special importance, for in addition to the usual mails in the ship's hold was a consignment of gold bullion, bound for London. No. 3440 was standing on the dockside with a five-vehicle train which was ideally suited to its power and capability and the mails and bullion were quickly loaded aboard. On the footplate was Inspector G.H. Flewellen, to oversee the working of the engine, and Driver Moses Clements, an experienced and highly-skilled engineman. Also aboard the train was noted train timer Charles Rous-Marten, a respected contributor to the railway press of the period on matters of locomotive speed and performance. The GWR was sharply aware of the importance of this particular train and was determined to put up a 'good show.'

At 9.23am that morning, less than 1¼ hrs after the liner had dropped anchor, Driver Clements was 'given the road' and he eased open the regulator to set his train in motion on what turned out to be a history-making trip. In partnership with his fireman, Clements hustled his train towards London in fine style, building up speed and momentum for the taxing climbs to Hemerdon and Dainton, reaching Exeter in less than an hour, at an average speed of nearly 56mph. With Exeter passed, Clements commenced the 20-mile climb to Whiteball Summit, beyond which he knew lay a downhill 'racing' section on which a significant burst of speed might be attempted. Fireman and driver clearly worked well together and the lengthy climb was covered at an average speed of 60mph, and Clements clearly did not ease the regulator after passing the summit, for *City of Truro* accelerated very rapidly indeed through Whiteball Tunnel and whisked its train down the bank which followed at truly breakneck pace. In the train, Rous-Marten timed the fastest quarter-mile at 8 ⅘ seconds — a speed of 102mph. To believe this, the reader has to accept that *City of Truro's* fastest acceleration occurred at the point at which the downward gradient was actually easing, which seems unlikely, but whether or not the magical 100mph was passed, *City of Truro's* performance was indeed startling. However, the GWR hierarchy did not share this view, and whilst before the event they had encouraged a good effort by Clements, they cannot have been prepared for what actually happened, and much consternation followed in the offices at Paddington. The event really ought to have been 'headline news' in both the daily newspapers and the railway press — but this did not happen. The 'Railway magazine' only alluded indirectly to the speed achieved, for the GWR was worried that published details of the escapade might terrify the travelling public away from its trains, especially since a serious accident at Preston in 1896, a result of high speed, was still fresh in the public mind.

Eventually, in 1922 — 18 years later — the GWR decided that the public at large was more accustomed to, and less alarmed by high speed rail travel and the *City of Truro* exploit of 1904 was finally given official recognition. Nevertheless, when in 1930 the engine was approaching the end of its working life, the GWR management did not consider the 4-4-0 to be of sufficient interest to warrant preservation and scrapping became a distinct possibility. Fortunately, GWR Chief Mechanical Engineer C.B. Collett recognised the historical value of the locomotive and in a furtive prompt, suggested to the LNER that it might offer the engine a home in the newly-established railway museum, in York. The LNER offer was duly made and accepted and No. 3440 *City of Truro* was despatched to York in 1931, where it took up residence in the Railway Museum. There it remained until January 1957, when No. 3440 emerged from the York Railway Museum to be returned to service for special duties. No. 3440 worked in this capacity until 1962, when it was installed in the newly-established GWR Railway Museum in Faringdon Road, Swindon. It appeared that this new Museum, located in a former Wesleyan chapel, was to be *City of Truro's* last resting place, but in July 1984 the 4-4-0 was transported by road to the Severn Valley Railway, where it was restored to main line running order in time for the 150th anniversary celebrations of the GWR, held in 1985.

Repainted in 1903-style livery, the locomotive returned to steam in time for the 1985 celebrations, during which it hauled passenger trains on both the SVR and also on BR main lines in former GWR territory, to considerable public acclaim. Since then, No. 3440 has been transferred to the National Railway Museum, and has worked excursions to Scarborough. This is one of the most appealing aspects of museum and private railway steam operation in the 1980s — working locomotives haul trains on main lines, pay working visits to private railways and also appear in museums, whose displays are consequently dynamic and varied. Casual visitors and enthusiasts alike are thus able to enjoy a changing panorama of considerable fascination.

Churchward played an important role in the development of the steam locomotive, by applying careful thought to the 19th century principles which had reached the peak of their development at the turn of the century. He was also not afraid to look beyond these shores, and adopted ideas from both France and America in his forward-thinking design work. He provided the foundations on which subsequent designers constructed many of their ideas and one of his trainees, William Stanier, developed basic Churchward principles to produce even greater achievements, following his appointment as CME of the mighty LMS, on January 1 1932.

The GWR was however best known for its use of the 4-6-0 type, built at Swindon over a period

of 54 years, for three different entities — the pre-Grouping GWR, the GWR of the 'Big Four' years and the Western Region of British Railways, which was still building ' Castle' 4-6-0s, virtually to the original drawings, 30 years after the first engine had rolled out of Swindon works! The four-cylinder 4-6-0 was the foundation of all GWR express passenger motive power for more than 40 years of new construction; on a wider scale it represented the zenith of steam locomotive development in the pre-First World War years.

Nevertheless, despite Churchward's pioneering nature, he was not the first British locomotive designer to use the 4-6-0 wheel arrangement. That honour had been claimed by Highland Railway CME David Jones, who in 1894 had introduced his 4-6-0 goods engine, a no-nonsense design which was successful from the outset. Jones displayed his confidence by ordering contractors Sharp Stewart to build 15 engines, from the original drawings. For an untried design, let alone a brand new concept, this was boldness indeed! Despite being classed as goods engines, the 4-6-0s probably worked in the mixed traffic capacity for which this particular wheel arrangement subsequently became so popular. By good fortune, HR No. 103 was preserved by the LMS and, after Nationalisation, the Scottish Region of British Railways restored the 4-6-0 to running order, painted it in the yellow ochre livery of the HR (which although very attractive, it probably never carried in service) and set the engine to work on excursion duties in 1955, in which capacity No. 103 served for nearly a decade. This magnificent engine survives today in the Glasgow Museum of Transport as a non-working exhibit, as a permanent reminder that Britain's most common mixed traffic locomotive type originated in the Highlands.

However, for all the boldness and style of the way in which Jones launched the 4-6-0 onto the British scene, it had little effect in inducing other railway companies to follow suit. Only mild interest was shown by other designers in the 4-6-0. On the North Eastern Railway, the 'S' class 4-6-0, designed as an express passenger engine, had appeared and whilst not particularly successful, it had pointed the way forward. No engines of this type survive in preservation.

On the GWR in the mid-1890s,, CME William Dean, although nearing the end of his tenure of office (1877-1902), appreciated that the 4-6-0 had great potential, and in 1896 he had built his own prototype, No. 36, followed by a second engine, No. 2601, in 1899. However, as might be expected, Dean's outlook was very much of the 'old school' and his 4-6-0s were cumbersome, ungainly, and included all manner of outdated features, including outside frames and wooden-centred bogie wheels. They were a new concept, built in the old idiom. Churchward however was quick to see what might be made of the 4-6-0 and, from the day of his appointment as CME of the GWR in 1902, it figured largely in the sweeping standardisation scheme already forming in his mind, though it is doubtful that at this early stage even he foresaw the full potential of his aims.

Whilst Churchward was a man of positive ideas, he was nevertheless determined to examine each avenue open to him, before selecting the option which best suited the needs of the Company. His pioneer 4-6-0, No.100 (later named *William Dean* as a tribute to his former chief) appeared as early as February 1902 (with two more 4-6-0s, Nos. 98 and 171 following in 1903) but he was aware of the work being carried out by engines of the 'Atlantic' type around the country and he commissioned his own trials to evaluate the type. In 1903, a small French-built De Glehn 'Compound' engine arrived in this country for trials on GWR metals,and following satisfactory performances, two larger De Glehn 'Atlantics' arrived in 1905. These engines worked alternate turns with the Churchward engines on main line duties from Paddington, thus giving

Churchward ample opportunity to compare performances.

Churchward remained open-minded about the 'Atlantic' type, and in 1905 built 13 examples of his own design, a simple expansion (rather than compound) two-cylinder engine, fitted with one of his standard taper boilers. A steam locomotive's capabilities can be judged on its ability to boil water, but the efficiency with which steam is used is also of vital significance, and Churchward's valve gear gave free passage for steam between boiler, cylinders and exhaust, producing a free-running engine capable of higher speed than might otherwise have been expected. Churchward had been particularly impressed however, with the sweeter-running produced by the multi-cylinder French engines and in 1906 constructed a four-cylinder simple 4-4-2, No. 40 *North Star*. Finally, in 1907 Churchward combined the sweet-running of a multi-cylinder design with his belief in six-coupled driving wheels to produce the first of his classic four-cylinder 4-6-0 classes — the ten 'Stars', Nos. 4001-10.

By this time, Churchward was convinced that future GWR motive power requirements would be best met by development of the 4-6-0, rather than the 'Atlantic.' Thus, in 1909, the four-cylinder 4-4-2 *North Star*, built in 1906, was converted as a 4-6-0 and in 1912-13 the Swindon-built two-cylinder 'Atlantics' of 1905 were also rebuilt as 4-6-0s — and the fact that the engines had been designed in the first place with this in mind says a great deal on the one hand about the CME's cautious perception of the future, and on the other about his determination to examine all options. Here indeed was a decision based on sound thought and careful experimentation. The GWR became committed to the 4-6-0 for its front line power, with simple engines driven by either two or four cylinders. So far as the 'Atlantic' was concerned, Churchward more than anyone else demonstrated that a well-designed, suitably proportioned 4-6-0 enjoyed up to 40 per cent greater adhesive weight on the rails, which helped performance considerably. Even so, development of the 'Atlantic' continued on other railways at this time, with ownership of about 300 engines spread over seven different companies, of which three were partners in the East Coast Main Line route to Scotland.

The GWR, having become committed to the 4-6-0, forged ahead with its development in both two and four-cylinder forms. The four-cylinder engines grew steadily greater in number as the Great War of 1914-18 approached, and by 1914 61 examples were in traffic — enabling the GWR

Above: The Great Central Railway, based at Lough-borough, in Leicester-shire, operates a passenger service over a five-mile section of the original GCR main line to London. Loughborough is thus an appropriate base for GCR 4-4-0 No. 506 *Butler Henderson,* a member of the National Collection maintained by the GCR under a loan agreement. No. 506 is seen here en-route from Loughborough to Rothley in winter sunshine on November 15 1986. *Mike Esau.*

Above: The celebrations held in 1985 to commemorate the 150th anniversary of the GWR were marked by an ambitious programme of the main line steam excursions over former GWR routes in the south west. On July 7 1985, 'Castle' 4-6-0 No. 5051 *Drysllwyn Castle* and 'Hall' No. 4930 *Hagley Hall* leave Newton Abbott with the 'Great Western Limited'. *Andrew Bell.*

to meet its wartime passenger requirements without having to resort to new construction at a difficult time. These engines were fitted with Churchward's magnificent boiler, incorporating features adopted from American practice which, at the time, gave the 4-6-0s a rather 'foreign' look from the British point of view. The conical tapering of the boiler from the rear was new to British observers, as was the high running plate with the curved plating beneath smokebox and cab — but how well they steamed! By marrying a sound boiler with multi-cylinder drive and valve gear which made the best of the boiler's output, Churchward created a locomotive that far outshone any of its contemporaries. No other British express engine of this era could steam and pull quite like a GWR four-cylinder 4-6-0: they would haul 480 tons steadily up a slight gradient for up to 20 minutes, at more than 60mph. Their reputation, and that of their designer, was justly earned in the rough-and-tumble of everyday service.

Having identified the 4-6-0 as its best option for front-line motive power in the years before 1910, the GWR thereafter never deviated from this course. Other railway companies experienced differing traffic patterns and motive power requirements, and it is of interest to examine the preserved engines from this era which we can still see in the 1980s to give an indication of how locomotives were developing elsewhere. For example, since the opening of the Great Central Railway's 'London extension' on March 15 1899, the company had relied for its passenger services on large 'Atlantic' and even 4-6-0 locomotives which were undeniably prestigious for the GCR, the last main line to be built into London. The large engines had been built in anticipation of rapidly increasing train weights, but GCR trains remained light in comparison to those of the other northbound main lines. A wider appreciation of the value of superheating steam in the early years of the 20th century paved the way for the construction of 4-4-0s capable of doing the work formerly done by larger 'Atlantic' type engines, and in 1913, GCR CME J.G. Robinson introduced his compact, inside-cylinder 'Director' 4-4-0s, which were soon hard at work, running capably and fast with the GCR's expresses from Marylebone to Manchester, Nottingham and Leicester. The first ten examples built in 1913 were all named after directors of the GCR, which was clearly happy with the class, for in 1919 the design was slightly enlarged and a further

11 locomotives of the 'Large Director' class were built. A further batch of 24 'Large Directors', modified specifically for service in Scotland with lower cabs and shorter chimneys, were built in 1924 by the LNER, which absorbed the GCR in the Grouping of 1923, and these latter engines were named after characters from Sir Walter Scott's novels.

'Large Director' No. 506 *Butler Henderson*, one of the engines built in 1919, now part of the National Collection and the sole survivor of the GCR's passenger classes, can be seen in the 1980s at work on the Great Central Railway, based at Loughborough, which operates passenger services to Rothley over a five-mile section of the former 'London extension'. This is indeed an appropriate home for the locomotive, which is painted in the glorious lined green livery of the GCR. *Butler Henderson* was withdrawn from service at Sheffield Darnall engine shed as BR No. 62660 in 1960 and was subsequently preserved in the Museum of British Transport, Clapham, London. This Museum closed in 1973, in preparation for the establishment of the National Railway Museum at York, which opened in 1975, and the historic 4-4-0 was loaned to the GCR, which restored it to working order.

Meanwhile, back on the GWR, no new passenger engines were built during the war, or for the first four years after the Armistice of November 1918. The first new front-line engines to appear from Swindon Works were the final 12 four-cylinder 'Stars', built in 1922/3 and named after famous Abbeys. Churchward, having established a strong and useful motive power plan for the GWR, retired in 1922 before the last batch of 'Stars' appeared, and was succeeded as CME by his long-time 'No. 2', Charles B. Collett. There was much continuity of approach at Swindon after the Grouping in motive power matters, but Collett enjoyed an important advantage always denied his predecessor, in respect of axle loadings. Churchward's designs had always been limited in the maximum axle load he could apply to his engines, as a result of weight restrictions imposed on underline structures by the GWR Civil Engineer. None of Churchward's engines exceeded an axle-loading of 19 tons. In Collett's time however, the civil engineering department finally authorised a 20-ton axle loading for locomotives — and this was not before time, for train weights were increasing and pre-1914 speeds and schedules were being reintroduced and even improved upon. Collett took advantage of the extra flexibility and in 1923 the first of his celebrated and much-loved four-cylinder 'Castle' 4-6-0s appeared — No. 4073 *Caerphilly Castle*, a locomotive now preserved as a non-working exhibit in the Science Museum, South Kensington.

Collett was able to give his 'Castles' a bigger firegrate, a bigger heating surface in the boiler and bigger cylinders to make better use of the increased steam output. With an axle load slightly within the new 20-ton limit, the new design was substantially more powerful than its predecessors and the 'Castles' evolved into one of the most successful and famous steam locomotive classes ever known, certainly in Britain and probably around the world. By 1950 a

Below: GWR 'Castle' 4-6-0s No. 5051 *Drysllwyn Castle* and 7029 *Clun Castle* at work near Highbridge, on Sunday September 8 1985 with a Plymouth-Bristol excursion during the GWR 150 celebrations.
Gavin Morrison.

total of 171 examples were in service and they were fleet-of-foot, efficient, and very popular with footplate crews. Speed records tumbled before them: in 1932 No. 5006 *Tregenna Castle* recorded the fastest ever start-to-stop run from Swindon to Paddington whilst hauling the 'Cheltenham Flyer' — running a distance of 77.3 miles at an average speed of 81.6mph, an incredible achievement for the era. Whenever preserved locomotives like No. 7029 *Clun Castle* or No. 5051 *Drysllwyn Castle* run on the main line today, they are proud reminders of some of the GWR's finest achievements in locomotive engineering and design. No. 5051 is normally resident at the Great Western Society's Didcot Railway Centre, whilst No. 7029 *Clun Castle's* home is the Birmingham Railway Musuem, Tyseley. Other surviving 'Castles' are listed in Chapter 9.

Nos. 5051 *Drysllwyn Castle* and 7029 *Clun Castle*, both illustrated in this book, provide interesting contrasts not only in the longevity of their design, but also in how they came to be preserved. No.5051 was completed at Swindon in May 1936 costing £4,848 to construct, of which the boiler accounted for £1,128! From 1936 to 1961 No. 5051 was allocated to the engine shed at Landore, South Wales, an unusually long stay for a 'Castle' of this vintage. From June

1961 to the end of 1962 the 4-6-0 was based at Neath before moving to Llanelly in February 1963. The engine was withdrawn from service in the following May and was sold to Woodham's of Barry for scrap on October 9 1963, after a working life of 27 years and 1,316,659 miles in revenue-earning service. The locomotive was privately purchased, for preservation by the Great Western Society, and the 4-6-0 was moved to Didcot in 1970, after seven years in the sidings at Barry Docks. Restoration was carried out by volunteers working mainly at weekends and this task occupied a ten year span — a tribute to the dedication and determination of steam volunteers. The locomotive was restored to gleaming working order by 1980, when No. 5051 represented the GWS at the celebrations held that year at Rainhill to commemorate the 150th anniversary of the opening of the Liverpool & Manchester Railway, the world's first railway built for the carriage of passengers. Since then the locomotive has performed regularly on main line excursions and it played a major part in the celebrations held in 1985 to mark the 150th anniversary of the GWR, hauling a variety of excursions over former GWR main lines in the south west. The locomotive has also been a major attraction at Didcot, where GWS visitors can enjoy short rides behind steam locomotives on the Centre's demonstration line. The GWS thus have helped to ensure that future generations can see and appreciate this important development of Churchward's ideas, first set in motion at the turn of the century.

The Birmingham Railway Museum, home of No. 7029 *Clun Castle*, has also contributed towards this worthy aim with its maintenance in main line running order of this BR-built 4-6-0. No. 7029 was one of the final batch of 'Castles' (Nos. 7028-37) built at Swindon by British Railways in May 1950. This batch, built virtually to the original specification, were modified only insofar as more modern lubrication and steam superheating equipment were fitted. No. 7029 performed the sad task of working the last steam-hauled train out of Paddington on June 11 1965. The locomotive ended its days as Gloucester station pilot, being withdrawn on December 31 1965 and was purchased straight from service by 7029 Clun Castle Ltd. This locomotive, in common with a number of sister 'Castles', was fitted in latter BR days with a double chimney, in which form the engine can be seen today. No. 7029 has also worked on main line railtours in addition to drawing the crowds to its home at the Birmingham Railway Museum, where it can be seen in steam at summer weekends and holiday times.

In their effect on subsequent locomotive development, the 'Castles' were the most significant motive power development in the years after the First World War. They were a logical extension of Churchward's work, but the GWR was nonetheless virtually alone in making any sort of real progress in advancing locomotive design generally. Other companies were supplementing their motive power needs through the construction of older pre-war types of 4-4-0, 4-6-0 and 0-6-0 configuration, most of which became increasingly inadequate in the face of heavier, faster traffic needs. The South Eastern & Chatham Railway and the London & South Western Railway had been making progress with 2-6-0, 2-6-4T and 4-6-0 types in the war years, but the overall trend was one of stagnation. The larger 'Pacific' type was in service already at this time with the GNR (subsequently LNER) but performance was not what might have been expected from such large engines, solely as a consequence of inferior valve gear, which made poor use of steam and prevented the engines running freely. Collett's 'Castle' 4-6-0s reigned supreme — at least for the moment.

On the SECR, and subsequently the Southern Railway, experience gained during the war with six-coupled types such as R.W. Urie's 20 powerful 'N15' class 4-6-0s of 1918 eventually led to the introduction of R.E.L. Maunsell's 'King Arthur' 4-6-0, as represented in preservation by No. 777 *Sir Lamiel*, owned by the National Railway Museum and maintained in main line running order by the Humberside Locomotive Preservation Group.

Below: On January 3 1987, Maunsell 4-6-0 No. 777 *Sir Lamiel* works steadily past Denham Golf Club with a main line 'Santa Special' train from Marylebone. *Peter Zabek.*

The 'King Arthurs' were developed from Urie's 'N15' class, which had not been performers of note, and the new engines were known in technical parlance as 'improved N15s' — hardly inspiring! At this time, the Southern Railway was suffering in the public view, for whilst in the eyes of the press the GWR excelled in all things, the SR was the butt of fairly relentless criticism. Thus, the SR Board of Directors appointed John Elliott, the Assistant Editor of the Evening Standard, as personal assistant to Sir Herbert Walker (the Company's General Manager), with responsibility for advertising and publicity. Elliott excelled at this and in his new position he imported (from the United States of America) the term Public Relations Officer, which was thus used in this country for the first time. He appreciated the value of good'PR' and persuaded the SR management and CME Maunsell that the new engines should have names associated with the legend of King Arthur and the Knights of the Round Table, in recognition of the Company's links with North Cornwall, the area traditionally linked with Camelot. The class of 74 engines all eventually carried evocative Arthurian names, giving them a positive identity with which passengers and the press could readily identify. However, embarrassment was only narrowly avoided when No. 767 was allocated the name of the traitor *Sir Mordred*! Happily, this was noticed in time and the engine eventually went into service as *Sir Valence*.

In service the 'King Arthurs' worked on the the boat trains between London Victoria and Dover, and on the West of England services, where they earned respect for good work on the difficult road between Salisbury and Exeter. They were versatile engines and at one time or other worked over most parts of the Southern system. The 'King Arthurs' were later displaced from their duties by the expanding electrification programme and in later years some examples were stored during the winter and were used only during the summer, when extra trains resulted in a shortage of motive power.

No.777 *Sir Lamiel*, the sole survivor of the class, was withdrawn in October 1961 and preserved as part of the National Collection. This was a lucky escape, for it had originally been intended to preserve No.30453 *King Arthur*, but a last minute change of plan consigned this engine to the scrapyard in favour of No. 30777. *Sir Lamiel* then spent 17 years in store before the National

Above: The Settle-Carlisle line in winter. On December 27 1984, SR 'King Arthur' 4-6-0 No. 777 *Sir Lamiel* crosses the towering arches of Ribblehead Viaduct in biting cold as it heads north with a 'Santa Steam Pullman' duty.
John Shuttleworth.

Above: SR 4-6-0 No. 850 *Lord Nelson* steams steadily northwards on the Settle-Carlisle line with an excursion working of February 25 1984. *Ian Smith.*

Facing page: The Settle-Carlisle line is a spectacular setting for main line steam excursions, featuring arduous climbs in both directions over the Pennines, to the lonely and windswept summit at Ais Gill. On March 3 1984, SR 4-6-0 No. 850 *Lord Nelson,* painted in bright malachite green SR livery, approaches Ais Gill from the north with a 'Cumbrian Mountain Pullman' duty. *John Cooper-Smith.*

Railway Museum accepted the Humberside team's offer to put the 4-6-0 back into steam. The 4-6-0 arrived at the HLPG's base in June 1978 and *Sir Lamiel* eventually had steam in its boiler again in 1982, 21 years after its grate had last carried a fire. The 4-6-0 subsequently made a successful return to main line service, mainly over routes in the north of England which it never visited in its working career.

Returning to the 1920s, in the wake of the 'King Arthur' came a locomotive which caused much consternation in the GWR offices at Paddington and Swindon. Whilst the two-cylinder 'King Arthurs' were capable machines, the steadily increasing demands of heavier and faster trains were stretching their capabilities. Thus, when the SR authorities announced an intention to run 500-ton expresses at an average speed of 55mph it was immediately apparent that new, more powerful locomotives were required. Maunsell considered the question carefully and in the light of the relative performances of the GWR 'Castles' and the LNER'S 'Pacifics' decided to construct a four-cylinder 4-6-0. The resulting class of 16 engines, whose pioneer was No. 850 *Lord Nelson*, was named after Naval commanders of great renown . . . evocative English names, such as *Sir Francis Drake, Howard of Effingham, Lord Hood* and *Sir John Hawkins.*

No. 850 emerged from the paintshop at Eastleigh works, near Southampton, in August 1926 and immediately caused consternation at Paddington, for in theoretical terms at least the SR locomotive was more powerful than Collett's 'Castle'. The SR joyously promoted its new claim to fame, much to the chagrin of GWR General Manager Sir Felix Pole. In service, the 'Lord Nelson' 4-6-0s proved capable of high power and fast running, but they required a greater degree of driving and firing skill than their versatile 'King Arthur' predecessors, and they were not universally liked as a result. Notwithstanding this, the 'Lord Nelson' class successfully worked the SR's heaviest express trains until Bulleid's controversial 'Merchant Navy' class 'Pacifics' arrived 16 years later. Even so, the 'Nelsons' continued to handle fast expresses to the end of their days with BR in the early 1960s. From 1959, the entire class of 16 engines was allocated to Eastleigh shed, where they remained until they disappeared from service in 1962. Their final duties were at the head of Waterloo-Southampton boat trains and Waterloo-Bournemouth express services. Sole survivor of the class, No. 30850 *Lord Nelson*, was withdrawn in August 1962 and preserved as part of the National Collection, the engine spending time thereafter in storage at Stratford (East London), Fratton, Preston Park (Brighton), Eastleigh and Tyseley. In the late 1970s, the National Railway Museum loaned *Lord Nelson* to Steamtown, Carnforth, where it was restored to main line running order in time for the Rainhill celebrations of 1980, where it appeared in the bright malachite green livery of the Southern Railway. Since then this locomotive has performed with a high degree of excellence on a wide variety of main line excursions.

The GWR's pride was deeply stung by the SR's claims about the 'Lord Nelson' 4-6-0s and Pole instructed Collett to reclaim for the GWR the honour of operating Britain's most powerful locomotive. He was aghast when he was told this could not be achieved! Collett reported that the 'Castle' 4-6-0s had been designed to the maximum axle loading the GWR's civil engineers would permit, and that a bigger engine could not be built. Pole was incensed. Not two years beforehand, Pole had been annoyed to discover that Collett had scrapped *The Great Bear*, Churchward's pioneer 'Pacific' of 1908 which although restricted in operational terms, was judged to be an immense asset in 'PR' terms. Viewed practically, Collett's decision had been correct: the 'Bear' needed a new boiler and he therefore shortened the frames and converted the engine into a 'Castle' 4-6-0 as No. 111 *Viscount Churchill*. Now, once again, the spectre of restricted axle-loading was returning to haunt Pole by giving the SR a competitive and promotional 'edge' of which the rival Company was quite naturally taking full advantage.

Accustomed to being supreme in all things, the GWR did not take kindly to being 'beaten at its own game' and Pole summoned Chief Civil Engineer J.C. LLoyd, and demanded an explanation. What he discovered amazed him, for Lloyd admitted that over the past 22 years, all new bridges on the main line to the west had been built to take an increased axle load of 22 tons, but being content with the extra flexibility and margins this granted, the bridge engineers had not bothered to appraise either the General Manager or CME about this uprating! As if this were not enough, Pole learned further that there were only four bridges on the entire route not yet uprated to the 22-ton standard. Under pressure from Pole, the civil engineers approved an increased 22½-tons axle load for four-cylinder engines by the summer of 1927 and Collett was ordered to have a bigger 4-6-0 of the highest power rating in the country ready for the same time. The CME's team settled down to enlarge and develop yet further their hallowed Churchward principles to produce the massive 'King' class 4-6-0s.

Below: The peak of GWR steam development was reached in 1927 with the construction of Collett's mighty 'King' class — the most powerful 4-6-0s ever to run in this country. No. 6000 *King George V*, owned by the National Railway Museum, is seen here nearing Sapperton Tunnel with a Swindon-Gloucester special of August 31 1985.
Hugh Ballantyne.

This class, as represented in the National Collection by class pioneer No. 6000 *King George V*, reclaimed for the GWR the privilege of operating the country's most powerful engine. The boiler was built to a new, bigger standard, the pressure was the highest yet at 250psi and Pole ordered that the first engine from the production line was to be shipped accross the Atlantic Ocean to fulfil the Company's commitment to exhibit an engine at the centenary display of the Baltimore & Ohio Railroad. With public relations firmly in mind, an early intention to name the class after English Cathedrals was abandoned in favour of English monarchs, and the 'Kings' were born.

The preserved No. 6000 was completed at great speed, in order that it could be properly 'run in' before being despatched to the United States and a determined team effort at Swindon saw the engine completed by the end of June 1927. Within three weeks the new engine was making its first appearance on the GWR's prestige 'Cornish Riviera' express, which was worked over the arduous South Devon routes for the first time without resort to double heading. On August 3, the engine was loaded aboard the SS *Chicago City* and shipped to America, where it impressed all observers with some very sharp running. At home, the 'Kings' proved to be complete masters of heavy trains; they accelerated purposefully with up to 500-tons coupled to the tender and could run at 70-75mph for long periods with these heavy loads. The class of 30 engines spent their entire lives, of more than 30 years, handling the heaviest express traffic.

From 1955, the class derived the benefit of research into performance and draughting, and the 'Kings' were all fitted with double chimneys by March 1958. They were the most powerful 4-6-0s ever built for use in Britain and for many years their home sheds were at Old Oak Common (London), Laira (Plymouth) and Wolverhampton (Stafford Road). Principal duties for the 'Kings' were the heavy expresses from Paddington to Bristol,Plymouth and Wolverhampton at the head of such crack expresses as 'The Bristolian,' the 'Cornish Riviera' and 'The Inter City.' The class was extinct by December 1962, No. 6000 *King George* V being withdrawn in December of that year, and acquired for preservation. The locomotive is now part of the National Collection and is based in main line running order at the Bulmer Railway Centre, Hereford, where the 4-6-0 still carries the commemorative bell from its American visit of 1927.

One of the most famous names popularly associated with steam locomotive history is 'The Royal Scot,' and this name was applied in 1927 both to the London Midland Scottish Railway's principal daily express from London to Scotland, and to a class of engines built to haul it. The name 'Royal Scot' is known to just about every man, woman and child in the country, but rarely has such a well-known locomotive class had such an unusual background. Survivors of this much-loved class include No. 6100 *Royal Scot*, preserved at the Bressingham Steam Museum, in Norfolk, and No. 6115 *Scots Guardsman*, based at the Dinting Railway Centre, near Manchester. Both engines have been steamed at their respective homes in recent years, while No. 6115 is also on BR's list of main line approved locomotives, though it has not worked a main line train in some years. The 'Royal Scot' 4-6-0s are still with us today (in rebuilt form) as a tangible reminder of a tangled and controversial period of railway history when rivalries were intense.

On the LMS, the biggest of the post-Grouping companies, rivalry between the principal factions, the former London & North Western Railway company at Crewe, and the former Midland Railway, at Derby, had led to stagnation in motive power development and by the middle of the decade the situation was acute. On the premier LMS Anglo-Scottish main line, from Euston to Carlisle and Glasgow, the existing 'Claughton' 4-6-0s, inherited from the LNWR, were increasingly unable to carry out their duties and a crisis was looming. The company's CME, Sir Henry Fowler, was considering the idea of a four-cylinder compound 'Pacific', whilst other factions within the Company felt that a 4-6-0 type was sufficient. Meanwhile, operations on the Anglo-Scottish main line were becoming worse by the day. So, in 1926, the LMS borrowed the GWR's No. 5000 *Launceston Castle* which was put to work on the West Coast Main Line. The results were astonishing. The engine immediately mastered its heavy trains on the Anglo-Scottish main line, only struggling when strong cross-winds in the Westmorland Fells blew sand off the rails in slippery conditions. Otherwise, so impressive was the engine at work over the steep banks in Westmorland and over Beattock, north of Carlisle, that the LMS made tentative enquiries about buying 50 'Castles' from Swindon! The GWR declined, and either refused or ignored a subsequent enquiry regarding the loan of a set of 'Castle' drawings. The LMS, in urgent need of new motive power and by now convinced that the 4-6-0 type best suited its needs, turned instead to the Southern Railway, where Maunsell was more amenable. He loaned a set of 'Lord Nelson' drawings' and whilst the LMS was impressed, the company decided to go for three, instead of four cylinder drive and ordered 50 engines 'straight off the drawing board' from the North British Locomotive Company, which was instructed to get on with the job as quickly as possible.

The first 'Royal Scot' engines were delivered within eight months of the order being placed and the whole batch of 50 engines was ready by mid-1927, to start hauling the new 'Royal Scot' express after which the class was named. The new train, a 15-coach formation weighing more than 415 tons, started operating on September 26 1927, hauled by the new class and running non-stop over the 301 miles between Euston and Carlisle. The principal Anglo-Scottish express had departed from Euston at 10am for many years, but this was the first time it had been named. It competed with the LNER's 'Flying Scotsman' express to Edinburgh, which left King's Cross each day at 10am, hauled by one of Nigel Gresley's 'Pacifics'.

As built, the 'Royal Scot' 4-6-0s were named after Scottish Regiments and pioneer locomotives of the LNWR, producing inspiring, attention-catching names such as *Black Watch, Lancashire Witch, The Old Contemptibles* and *The Lancer*. In the 1930s, the pioneer engine names were replaced by more regimental names. The naming of the class in itself was something of a new departure for the LMS, for after the Grouping the new company's management had announced that whilst existing named classes would retain their names, no new names would be allocated. Clearly, by 1927, the image of Gresley's named 'Pacifics' on the LNER and Elliot's clever and successful 'PR' on the Southern Railway involving the 'Lord Nelson' and 'King Arthur' 4-6-0s had been duly noted and acted upon at Euston. The introduction of 'The Royal Scot' express in 1927 marked the beginnings of a fresh start for the LMS, where the rate of progress and

development increased even more following the appointment of William Stanier, from the GWR, as CME in 1932.

The 'Royal Scots' gave the LMS the engines it needed at a difficult time in the Cmpany's history, and the class of hastily-built 4-6-0s capably handled the Anglo-Scottish express traffic for about five years. The 'Scots' reigned supreme on the West Coast Main Line until 1933, when Stanier's 'Pacifics' were introduced, but the 4-6-0s retained an important role on Anglo-Scottish traffic from Euston and other passenger duties for the remainder of their life on the LMS, and also for BR, virtually to the end of everyday steam traction on the national network. From 1943 to 1955 the class was progressively rebuilt with more modern taper boilers to replace the original parallel barrel variety, and the class regularly appeared in charge of prestige trains such as 'The Thames Clyde Express', 'The Red Rose', 'The Irish Mail', and 'The Mancunian.'

The two preserved engines, No. 6100 and No. 6115, survive in rebuilt form: No. 6100 was withdrawn in October 1962 whilst No. 6115 had the honour of being the last of its class to work in service for BR, and was latterly much in demand for railtours and special trains. It was withdrawn in December 1965. Class pioneer No. 6100 *Royal Scot* was withdrawn from service at Nottingham in October 1962 as BR No. 46100 and was subsequently preserved and stored at

Above: The pre-National-isation era recreated on the Bluebell Railway, in Sussex, as 'Schools' class 4-4-0 No. 928 *Stowe* hauls a passenger train on the five-mile line between Sheffield Park and Horsted Keynes, on September 15 1985. *Mike Esau.*

Crewe works. The locomotive was purchased by Butlins Ltd and was displayed in the open at their Skegness holiday camp until transfer to the Bressignham Steam Museum in 1971, where it is preserved today in crimson lake livery — which it never carried in rebuilt form.

The general trend in the late 1920s was of increasing size — it might thus come as something of a surprise to note that right at the end of the decade the classic British passenger engine of previous years, the 4-4-0, made a comeback. And what a comeback! On the SR, CME Maunsell produced his 'Schools' class of engines — the most powerful 4-4-0 ever to run in this country.

The 1920s were difficult years for the Southern Railway. Quite apart from the problems arising out of the aftermath of the war, with a run-down fleet of old engines facing an increasingly difficult work-load for which they were not ideally suited, the SR had to contend with a number of other internal struggles. That these internal wrangles did not develop into the sort of bitterness which affected the LMS at this time is a credit to the Company's management, but it nevertheless made life difficult for CME Maunsell and his staff. In addition to the difficulties of making the formerly independent pre-Grouping constituents work well together, Maunsell also had to contend with expanding electrification. The two-cylinder 'King Arthurs' of 1924 had been followed by the four-cylinder 'Lord Nelson' 4-6-0s to satisfy the operators needs for a more powerful engine, now Maunsell was asked for another fast, powerful engine to work the difficult, secondary main lines such as Tonbridge-Hastings and Woking-Portsmouth. These routes were sinuous, steeply graded, and featured very narrow tunnels, especially on the Hastings line. The engines required needed to be powerful and fast, yet at the same time compact in both length and width.

Maunsell first considered a cut-down 'Lord Nelson', using as many standard parts as possible to keep costs down, but problems with excessive weight made this scheme impossible to implement. The 'Schools' class therefore emerged as a smaller version of the popular 'King Arthur' 4-6-0 of 1924, though fitted with three cylinders, compared with the four-cylinder drive of the 'Nelson' and the two cylinders of the 'Arthur.' It was a marvellous compromise which enabled the new design to competently fulfil the requirements of the traffic department. The round-topped boiler derived from the 'Arthur' allowed the provision on the 'Schools' of the

narrow-topped cab needed for the very restricted tunnels of the Hastings line, while the 4-4-0 configuration gave smooth running on the twisting track. The large boiler provided ample steam and the three-cylinder drive was confident, powerful and capable of producing very high speed. The 'Schools' were a great success. They mastered and dominated the east Kent express turns in the 1930s, and even ran from London to Bournemouth and Portsmouth, where some sparkling performances were recorded.

The class was still handling heavy, express passenger trains in 1960, by which time the writing was clearly on the wall for British steam: the BR Modernisation Plan had been announced and implemented five years before and large numbers of new diesels were appearing at a steady rate to displace steam traction. On the SR, the ever-advancing tide of electrification provided a second threat to Stephenson's creation. In 1960, the Kent Coast electrification displaced and prompted withdrawal of the first examples of the 40-strong 'Schools' class and within two years the splendid breed was extinct. Of the preserved examples, No. 30928 *Stowe* (built 1934) was the first to be withdrawn, from Brighton shed, in December 1962, after which it was bought by Lord Montagu for static display, with a trio of Pullman cars, in the grounds of the National Motor Museum, at Beaulieu. The 4-4-0 was transported to Eastleigh Works in 1973 for restoration in SR green livery and moved thereafter to the East Somerset Railway, at Cranmore. *Stowe* moved to the Bluebell Railway on loan in 1980 and re-entered service in 1981, to run between Sheffield Park and Horsted Keynes.

Nos. 30925 *Cheltenham* and 30926 *Repton* were both withdrawn in December 1962. No. 30925 is based at the National Railway Museum and appeared in steam at the 150th anniversary celebrations of the Liverpool & Manchester Railway in 1980. No. 30926 was exported to the USA shortly after withdrawal, and it is still seen in steam occasionally.

The 4-4-0 reached its zenith with Maunsell's magnificent 'Schools' class of 1930. Built for a special need, the class utilised the experience gained through the trend towards bigger locomotives of the 4-6-0 configuration to produce a successful compromise which was not only popular with its crews, but very powerful and, when the opportunity arose, very fast. The Bluebell Railway is currently the only place in the country where an example of this superb class can be seen in steam and working trains. Whilst the static museum has a major role in the display and interpretation of our railway history, the work of institutions like the Bluebell

Railway, which depend so much on voluntary effort and goodwill for their development, is of great value.

The 4-4-0 also made a comeback on the LNER in 1927, when Nigel Gresley introduced his three-cylinder 'D49' class. Pioneer engine of the class was LNER No. 234 Yorkshire, completed at Darlington in September of that year. Designed for intermediate passenger work, the class, which eventually numbered 76 examples, were all named after counties served by the LNER, and were thus known generally as 'Shires.' Following Nationalisation the class was renumbered in the 627xx series and a sole example of this well-proportioned class survives at Falkirk, in the hands of the Scottish Railway Preservation Society. The engine, Morayshire, carries the rich apple green livery and No. 246 of the LNER, trimmed in white and black lining. The locomotive was taken out of BR serice in 1961 and was bought by Scottish steam enthusiast Ian Fraser. Morayshire was restored at Inverurie Works in 1964 and presented to Edinburgh's Royal Scottish Museum in 1966. Subsequently loaned to the Scottish Railway Preservation Society in 1975, the 4-4-0 was restored to working order at the SRPS base at Falkirk, where it is based today as main line approved locomotive.

Appropriately, at the close of the decade the Gresley 'Shire' and Maunsell 'Schools 4-4-0s represented the end of one logical area of steam locomotive development, for the overall trend was generally towards bigger locomotives of greater power. On the LNER, Gresley's 'Pacifics' had been at work for some time, whilst on the Southern, Maunsell had also produced the 'King Arthur and 'Lord Nelson' 4-6-0s. On the GWR Collett had developed Churchward's work to the ultimate conclusion to produce the swift 'Castle' and mighty 'King' 4-6-0s, whilst the LMS, after a turbulent period of intrigue and gestation, was doing well with its 'Royal Scot' 4-6-0s, all of which can be appreciated today at private railways, in railway centres or in Museums. These engines are the evocative reminders of a particularly significant period of railway history, for as the 1920s became the 1930s, Britain's railways were entering their truly golden age — the era of the big engine and more spectacularly, the age of the 'streamliners.'

Below: An impressive image of GWR achievement of the 1920s, as 'Castle' No. 7029 *Clun Castle,* one of the BR-built engines of 1950, leads 'Hall' No. 4930 *Hagley Hall* at Pontrilas with 'The Western Stalwart' main line special, from Cardiff to Hereford, on July 6 1985. *Andrew Bell.*

CHAPTER 4:
ZENITH OF STEAM

Above: William Stanier's finest creation — the 'Princess Coronation' class 'Pacific'. This is BR No. 46229 *Duchess of Hamilton*, maintained in main line running order by the Friends of the National Railway Museum, and pictured here at Steamtown, Carnforth, on April 10 1982.
Peter J.C. Skelton.

By the late 1920s, the lead in locomotive design established by Churchward on the GWR had been significantly eroded and across the country, engineers from other companies appreciated much more fully the 'why and wherefore' of efficient operation in a variety of technical areas. For example, valve gears making full use of the expansive properties of steam became more widespread, resulting in free-running locomotives making more efficient use of coal and water. The GWR's lead finally disappeared altogether after 1930, when Gresley and Stanier created steam locomotives of unprecedented appearance, power and speed. In the 1930s, the British steam locomotive reached the pinnacle of development and performance, when sound design and high-quality construction were matched with second-to-none handling, and a maintenance programme which gave the locomotives a high degree of availability. Competition between the 'Big Four' companies and an intense pride in their work created a team spirit and quality of operation amongst railwaymen in this decade which resulted in substantial advances in speed, efficiency and time-keeping. These were truly the 'golden years' of the steam locomotive in the 20th century, and there are some very famous survivors to illustrate the individual chapters of this exciting story.

   Probably the most famous preserved main line steam locomotive of them all is Sir Nigel Gresley's 'A3' class 'Pacific' No. 4472 *Flying Scotsman*, owned today by the Hon. W.H.McAlpine, who maintains the locomotive in working order. Built in 1923 and withdrawn from service after 40 years at work in 1963, *Flying Scotsman* continues to delight thousands of people when it appears at the head of a main line excursion. In 1986, the apple green-liveried 4-6-2 appeared frequently on British Rail's hugely successful programme of special trains operated between Marylebone and Stratford upon Avon, hauling heavy trains over a steeply graded line, up to BR's maximum permitted speed of 60mph for steam locomotives. A creditable record for a locomotive then in its 63rd year! No. 4472 *Flying Scotsman* represents an important milestone in locomotive development generally and for the East Coast main line in particular, for Nigel Gresley's 'Pacifics' took over the glamorous prestige role inaugurated on the East Coast Main Line by Patrick Stirling's 'Singles' and held in the early part of the 20th century by Ivatt's fiery 'Atlantics.' *Flying Scotsman* thus enables us to trace the thread of locomotive development a stage further, leading to the introduction in 1935 of Gresley's splendid 'A4' class streamlined 'Pacifics', including No. 4468 *Mallard*, which is maintained in the mid-1980s in working order by the National Railway Museum. *Mallard* gained immortality on July 3 1938, when a short sprint at 126mph established a world speed record for steam traction which stands unchallenged today.

H.N.Gresley had been appointed as Chief Mechanical Engineer of the Great Northern Railway in 1911, and it had thus fallen to him to oversee the motive power requirements of the East Coast Main Line during the First World War. The '251' class 'Atlantics' introduced by H.A. Ivatt in 1902 were capable of fine work, and Gresley's subsequent modifications to the design included the fitting of high-degree superheaters, by which the steam generated in the boiler was heated a second time in the heat from the fire, to produce intensely hot, dry steam, which could be used much more efficiently than the 'wet' steam initially produced by a locomotive boiler. Gresley also fitted the Ivatt 'Atlantics' with larger, more efficient cylinders and piston valves (which distribute the steam to the pistons) and whilst appearance was little changed, performance was transformed. In later years they were capable of deputising for Gresley's larger 'Pacifics' on the heaviest, most exacting duties. For example, following a 'Pacific' failure at Grantham, a modified '251' 'Atlantic' whisked the afternoon 'Flying Scotsman' from Grantham to York (82¾ miles) in 86½ minutes, hauling an enormous train of 17 coaches, weighing 585 tons.

Notwithstanding such spectacular performances, it was clear to Gresley that the 'Atlantics' were fully extended and that bigger, more powerful locomotives were required. He thus started work on his first 'Pacific' design, the 'A1' class locomotives introduced by the Great Northern Railway in 1922, on the very eve of the Grouping, thereby giving the GNR another important place in the historical evolution of the steam locomotive. The arrival of Gresley's 4-6-2s of 1922

Below: No. 4472 *Flying Scotsman*, the first British steam locomotive to record a formally authenticated speed of 100mph (in 1934), passes Buxworth on November 10 1984 with 'The Fenman' excursion. *Chris Milner.*

47

marked the start of a new era in locomotive development, for they were the first successful class of British 'Pacifics.'

The first two 'A1s' were Nos. 1470, subsequently named *Great Northern* and 1471 *Sir Frederick Banbury*. In designing the 'A1', Gresley took care not to repeat the GWR's mistake, as evidenced by *The Great Bear* (See Chapter 3) in producing a locomotive whose excessive length and weight restricted its sphere of operations, and his first 'Pacifics' represented a marked and useful increase in power and capacity over their 'Atlantic' predecessors. The engines were powerful and on Sunday September 3 1922, No. 1471, at that stage still un-named, hauled a special test train of 20 vehicles (weighing 610 tons) over the 105.5 miles of main line from King's Cross to Grantham in 122 minutes, at an average speed of 70mph. This time was only two minutes longer than the 'Flying Scotsman' schedule of 1950! The third 'A1' to take shape in the Doncaster works erecting shop was No. 1472 *Flying Scotsman*, but the Grouping took place before the locomotive was completed: it therefore entered service as LNER No. 4472 in January 1923. In simple physical terms, and indeed in their power rating, the 'A1' class 4-6-2s were the most powerful engines in the country and the LNER was justly proud of Gresley's new design. But there was a profound shock just around the corner.

In 1923, C.B. Collett's superb 'Castle' class 4-6-0s appeared on the GWR, which in theoretical terms were more powerful than Gresley's new 'Pacifics.' Partisan claim and counter-claim followed and in 1924, at the British Empire Exhibition staged at Wembley, the immaculately groomed No. 4472 *Flying Scotsman* stood close to the GWR's No. 4073 *Caerphilly Castle*. The GWR's publicity department made sure that visitors to the Exhibition were made aware that their 4-6-0, physically the smaller of the two engines, was the most powerful locomotive in the country, in terms of tractive effort. The LNER was stung, but quite how the interchange trial which followed actually came about has never been made clear. When Gresley discovered that a 'Castle' and an 'A1' were to be the subject of comparative testing on the two companies' main lines from Kings Cross and Paddington, he is reported to have been angry — but the instruction came from a very senior level and the die was cast. Perhaps the contest was the result of an after-dinner conversation between Board members, in a smoke-filled room during or shortly after the Wembley exhibition. We shall never know for certain, but between April 27 and May 2 1925, 'A1' No. 4474 *Victor Wild* and 'Castle' No. 4079 *Pendennis Castle* ran on the main lines of their opposite companies, and much passion, partisanship and prominent press coverage sparked an atmosphere of almost gladiatorial competition.

On the GWR, the lengthy LNER 'Pacific' was not especially well-suited to the hilly, highly curvacious nature of the South Devon banks for which the GWR 4-6-0s had been specifically designed, but the LNER crew nevertheless performed well in the circumstances. The GWR, 'pulling out all the stops', turned in some spectacular performances, including bringing in the 'Cornish Riviera Limited' up to 15 minutes early! As newcomers to the route, the LNER engine and crew therefore performed adequately from Paddington — after all, it was only to be expected that the 'home team' would do well. However, in the running from Kings Cross, where the 'A1s' ought to have done well, the GWR 'Castle' mastered every train, out-performing the Gresley 'Pacific' in many respects, and leaving the LNER authorities open-mouthed in astonishment at the ease which the 4-6-0 confidently accelerated away from King's Cross with trains weighing nearly 500 tons. Prior to the event, the LNER had been quietly confident that this relatively small 4-6-0 would struggle on the difficult start from the London terminus, and slip to a stand even before Gas Works Tunnel, just a few yards from the platform ends on the stiff gradient from King's Cross station. LNER pride was deflated quickly, undisputedly and in a very public fashion.

Controversy and a deal of bad feeling between the GWR and LNER surrounded the outcome and published results of the trials, which received very extensive media coverage. The GWR's 'edge' in the interchange trials had been in its utilisation of a higher boiler pressure of 220psi (compared with the 180psi of the Gresley locomotives) in conjunction with long travel piston valves, which afforded minimal restriction to the steam in its passage in and out of the cylinders, encouraging free-running and giving much greater efficiency. The lower pressure of the 'A1' boilers and the short-travel valve gear, which effectively throttled the steam supply to the cylinders, were weaknesses which the 'Castle' performance put into very sharp focus. In fairness, Gresley's supporters have claimed that he was aware of the shortcomings of his 'A1s' in this respect, and that he had planned in any case to experiment and adapt gradually in the direction of longer valve travel as the years passed. Following this line of thought, the 1925 trials simply interposed and highlighted in a very embarrassing fashion a problem which was already understood and under review. However, long valve travel and higher boiler pressures became standard practice on the LNER after 1925.

As the 1920s progressed, Gresley carried out careful experiments with higher boiler pressures, leading to a general rebuilding and uprating of the 'A1' class, which were all subsequently fitted with higher pressure boilers and smaller diameter cylinders as class 'A3'. With these refinements, the 'A3s' became engines *par excellence* — powerful, fast, economical and popular with their crews.

As recounted in Chapter 3, the LNER and the LMS had been competing with each other for the prestige Anglo-Scottish passenger traffic since the late 19th century, and in the late 1920s there was a further flurry of activity. The introduction of the new 'Royal Scot' stock and locomotives by the LMS prompted the LNER to make bold plans to inaugurate non-stop running

for the 'Flying Scotsman' over the entire 392¾ miles between King's Cross and Edinburgh. However, it would have been too much to expect a single footplate crew to work such an arduous shift, so Gresley designed a 'corridor tender' incorporating a gangway connection, giving access to the leading coach. A second engine crew, travelling in a reserved compartment at the front of the train, could gain access to the footplate through a cramped corridor down the right-hand side of the tender, to take their turn on the footplate. The crew taking the non-stop 'Flying Scotsman' from King's Cross usually left the footplate just north of York, leaving the second crew to take the train on to Edinburgh.

The non-stop service started on May 1 1928, when No. 4472 *Flying Scotsman* hauled the inaugural service from King's Cross. This was an age of competition and rivalry, and the LMS stole some of the glory from the LNER on Friday, April 27 1928 prior to the Monday on which the non-stop 'Flying Scotsman' was due to start. The Euston hierarchy arranged for Midland Railway 'Compound' 4-4-0 No. 1054 to be fitted with coal rails around the tender top, allowing extra coal to be carried, and together with the 'Scot' No. 6113 *Cameronian* ran the 'Royal Scot' in two portions, non-stop, to both Glasgow (No. 6113) and Edinburgh (No. 1054). This was a publicity-seeking 'one-off' and the LNER rightfully earned the credit, for at the time of its introduction the 'Flying Scotsman' was the longest non-stop railway passenger service in the world.

Because of the long-standing agreement with the West Coast route operator, now the LMS, not to run a London-Edinburgh service in less than 8¼hrs, the average speed of the new service did not exceed 47½mph, which was slow, even for those days. Booked to leave King's Cross daily at 10.00am, arrival in Edinburgh was not due until 6.15pm. In order to compensate for the long journey time, and perhaps to distract passengers from noticing the relatively low speed, new restaurant facilities were introduced, together with other services such as an on-train hairdressing salon. The LNER managers carefully stage-managed the inauguration of the new non-stop service, especially in the face of competition from the LMS, and in early 1928 the company had actually denied rumours of imminent non-stop running from London to Edinburgh. Instead, the LNER had merely stated that the forthcoming summer services "were yet to be considered." The Board did not wish to lessen the impact of the new service and therefore tried hard to throw the press 'off the scent.'

No. 4472 *Flying Scotsman* therefore played an important role in the LNER's new non-stop 'Flying Scotsman' service from the very start, in May 1928. In 1932, the tiresome 8¼hrs limit on King's Cross-Edinburgh services was finally abandoned, by mutual agreement with the LMS, permitting a long-overdue acceleration in journey times. No. 4472 was then 'in the news' again in 1934, during trials to assess the possibility of even higher speed running between King's Cross and Newcastle in 4 hrs on a regular basis. With 147 tons on the tender drawbar, including the LNER dynamometer car for accurate measurement of speed and performance, and running to Leeds rather than Newcastle, *Flying Scotsman* was allowed 165 minutes for the 185.7 mile

journey. Arriving at Leeds 13 minutes early, the 4-6-2 established new records for this line, and on the return journey, with two extra coaches added, No. 4472 was spurred to even greater achievement, and became the first British steam locomotive to record the first properly authenticated 100mph. GWR 4-4-0 No. 3440 *City of Truro's* long-disputed 100mph run of 1904 (see Chapter 3) was finally and formally superseded, giving No. 4472 *Flying Scotsman* another important historical 'first.'

Following Nationalisation in 1948, No. 4472 became BR No. 60103, which was withdrawn from service in 1963 and purchased by businessman Alan Pegler. The engine was maintained in working order and in 1968, to commemorate the 40th anniversary of the inaugural run of the non-stop 'Flying Scotsman' , the engine worked once again, without stopping, from London to Edinburgh. In 1969, No. 4472 was shipped to the United States of America, to haul a British trade exhibition train, for which the locomotive was fitted with a headlamp and bell in accordance with American operating practice. Following the end of everyday steam traction in this country in August 1968, BR had imposed a ban on the operation of steam engines over its tracks, and the American tour would at least allow the locomotive to run at reasonable main line speeds.

The first part of the tour, during a six-week period in late 1969, covered 2,200 miles of railway in the south eastern states, with a nine-coach train promoting British goods and services. Approximately 56,000 people visited the train, but the venture was not a financial success, and a second tour the following year suffered the same fate. Sadly, Alan Pegler, who had invested so much in time, money and effort to preserve *Flying Scotsman* was bankrupted by the venture and No. 4472 was stranded in America. The locomotive might still be there today, but for the efforts of the Hon. W.H.McAlpine, who bought No. 4472 and shipped the engine back home. The 4-6-2, complete with the second tender attached after preservation to increase its water capacity, was unloaded from the ship *California Star* in Liverpool docks in February 1973. *Flying Scotsman* was subsequently overhauled and repainted in LNER apple green livery and put back to work, and the engine still appears regularly on main line trains. It is indeed a locomotive with an important past and a fascinating history.

The 1934 high speed runs with No. 4472 between London and Leeds had proved that a 4hr timing between Newcastle and King's Cross was a realistic possibility using the 'A3s', or 'Super Pacifics' as they were known at the time. However, in Germany a streamlined diesel train, known as the 'Flying Hamburger' was receiving much media attention. High speed rail traction was also attracting headlines in America and railways throughout Britain and the world became rapidly aware of the high public profile and popularity generated by high-speed running. Streamlining was very much in vogue at this time, but the LNER believed it could match the diesel's speed and performance using steam, fuelled by British coal rather than expensive, imported fuel oil. Thus encouraged, the CME's team, which included future SR CME O.V.S.Bulleid as Gresley's 'No. 2', produced the magnificent 'A4' class 4-6-2.

Above: The fastest steam locomotive in the world — the National Railway Museum's Gresley 'A4' No. 4468 *Mallard* forges up Hatton Bank on November 8 1986 with 'The Peter Allen Pullman', en-route from Marylebone to York. No. 4468 is painted in LNER garter blue livery, with nameplates replacing painted names, and retaining the deep valances over the wheels. *W.A. Sharman.*

Left: No. 4498 *Sir Nigel Gresley* accelerates south from Appleby, on the Settle-Carlisle line, with a 'Cumbrian Mountain Express' train in February 1980. Note how the wheel valances were subsequently modified, compared with the picture above, to facilitate access for maintenance. The 'A4' cabs were comfortable for the footplate crew, who were even provided with upholstered 'bucket' seats for their long journeys!
Steve Le Cheminant.

In performance terms, the 'A4' was a logical extension of the 'A3', featuring a still higher steam pressure of 250psi, and the steam passages and valve gear were carefully designed to use the steam as efficiently and powerfully as possible. But it was the appearance of the 'A4' class which made a tremendous impact. Nothing like these beautiful streamlined creatures had ever been seen before: the aerofoil curve of the running plate from front to rear, the wind-cutting wedge-shaped front end and the valances concealing roughly half the depth of the wheels was something completely new in British practice, and the 'A4s' were rightly promoted as 'the wonder of the age'. In colour too they were different, the first four engines of the class being painted in shades of light grey and black and named *Silver Link, Silver King, Silver Fox and Quicksilver*. Fitted with chime whistles which gave a melodious, although slightly ghostly sound, the 'A4s' were utterly stunning. The streamlined casing was carefully designed to reduce wind resistance but it also had a remarkable effect on the travelling British public and railway observers. The LNER acquired a sleek, speedy and streamlined image and a reputation for being modern and up-to-date.

Above: A pleasing broadside view of Scottish-based 'A4' No. 60009 *Union of South Africa*, which has been maintained in the lined Brunswick green livery applied to this class by BR after 1948. Known to enthusiasts simply as 'No. 9', the 4-6-2 is seen here running 'light engine' towards Carnforth on March 31 1984, in connection with a 'Cumbrian Mountain Express' working. *Trevor Davey*.

The LNER announced that the new engines would haul a new train, the 'Silver Jubilee', an express named to commemorate the 25th anniversary of the coronation of King George V, and the new coaches were designed to match the locomotive. They were finished in a striking aluminium colour, with bellows between the coaches to reduce wind resistance and 'skirts' which almost came down to rail level. The effect of the whole train was quite startling. After a period of running in, No. 2509 *Silver Link* hauled an inaugural 'Silver Jubilee' special from King's Cross to Grantham and return, with invited press guests on board, on Friday September 27 1935. The crew were clearly under instructions to put on a 'good show' and the main line was kept clear in front of Gresley's new creation as it left King's Cross with its train of VIPs. As *Silver Link's* speed increased, records tumbled. It established a new British record for steam traction with a maximum speed of 112½mph and averaged 107.5mph for 25 miles, running at 100 mph continuously for approximately 43 miles. Gresley was delighted, and Driver Taylor and Fireman Luty rounded-off the 'down' trip by arriving at Grantham 10 minutes early. This marvellous debut clearly illustrated the speed capability and reserve of the 'A4', for such demanding speeds were not required in everyday service. The 'Silver Jubilee' was nevertheless booked to run from King's Cross to Newcastle (232¼ miles) in 4hrs, requiring an average speed of 70mph, and a maximum speed of 90mph for considerable distances. Sadly, pioneer 'A4' *Silver Link* is with us no more: renumbered 60014 by the British Railways organisation in 1948, the locomotive worked in top link main line service until December 1962, when it was withdrawn. The 'Pacific' was

52

Left: The gleaming copper and brass pipework and fittings in the cab of No. 4468 *Mallard* as viewed from the drivers side of the cab. It was once the ambition of every schoolboy to drive express steam locomotives — and this is still possible today on the preserved railways of this country! *Chris Milner.*

Below: The chime whistle mounted in front of the chimney is blowing as No. 60009 *Union of South Africa* rounds the curves in Barons Wood, on the Settle-Carlisle line, with a 'Cumbrian Mountain Express' of April 24 1984. *Peter J.C. Skelton.*

dismantled for scrap at Doncaster works in August 1963.

The 'A4s' easily mastered their duties on the East Coast Main Line between London and Scotland and between 1935 and 1938 a total of 35 examples were built at Doncaster. The 'Silver Jubilee' was immediately successful and the LNER looked for new ways of expanding on the popular high-speed express service it could now operate. The coronation in 1937 of King George VI provided the opportunity and the 'Coronation' express linking London with Edinburgh was born. The LNER aimed to provide a 6hr service over the 393-miles route — 2¼hrs less than the 'Flying Scotsman' schedule for the same route only five years before! The down 'Coronation' was booked to run at a start-to-stop average of 71.9mph between King's Cross and York, thereby beating the 71.4mph rating of the GWR's 'Cheltenham Flyer' over the much easier route between Swindon and Paddington.

The LNER was thus gaining much valuable experience of high speed running with its new, sleek, and very fast engines. Competition with the LMS was in the air once again, not just for the Anglo-Scottish traffic, but also for speed records, and whilst the LMS held the crown briefly in June 1937 (114mph), 'A4' No. 4468 *Mallard* became the fastet steam locomotive in the world on July 3 1938 when it streaked down Stoke Bank at 126mph, during a series of brake test trials. The record stands unchallenged in the 1980s and is unlikely ever to be broken. A commemorative plaque was fitted, which is still mounted on the boiler cladding today. After withdrawal as BR No. 60022 in April 1963, *Mallard* was restored as completely as possible to its condition during the record breaking year of 1938, after which it was displayed at the Museum of British Transport, Clapham. It was moved to York following the establishment of the National Railway Museum, where it was displayed in the Main Hall as a static exhibit for a decade.

In 1985, *Mallard* was restored to main line running order, with financial assistance from the borough of Scarborough, destination of many summer steam excursions from York, and the distinguished locomotive had steam in its boiler again in time for the NRM's tenth anniversary, in 1985. Since then the engine has appeared on a number of main line excursions, including the Marylebone-Stratford trains.

Appointed as CME of the LMS in 1932, William Stanier's mandate was to produce a range of standard classes having a maximum number of interchangeable parts, and to a railway plagued for a decade by factional dispute, he brought a calculated and sensible approach which had nothing to do with pre-Grouping loyalty to any of the LMS constituents. Possibly his best known design, and certainly the most numerous, was the mixed traffic class 5 4-6-0, dealt with in Chapter 5. However, in the field of express passenger traction, he left three classes of which examples can still be seen running today.

William Stanier was working for the GWR as C.B. Collett's assistant when he was offered the post of CME by the LMS, a proposal which astonished him. Stanier was only a few years younger than Collett and realised that if he was offered the post of CME for the GWR at all, he would have only the briefest tenure of office. There was sound thinking behind the LMS Board's choice for the Directors were worried that there would be a recurrence of factional rivalry if an LMS engineer of pre-Grouping background were appointed as CME, and the Board preferred to look outside the Company. Equally importantly, the LMS had not forgotten the spectacular performances recorded by the 'Castle' 4-6-0 over the West Coast Main Line in the autumn of 1926, or the fact that the GWR had been unwilling to impart any of its secrets by lending a set of drawings prior to the construction of the 'Royal Scot' 4-6-0s. Employing a Swindon-trained locomotive designer as CME, who would bring with him the specialist knowledge he had gained, was thus of significant appeal to the LMS Board!

When Stanier came to the LMS on January 1 1932, the 70 'Royal Scot' 4-6-0s were the only bright spot in a very murky pool of main line motive power. Generally speaking, front line motive power on the LMS was old, outmoded and increasingly inadequate. Unlike Collett, on the GWR, whose succession to the office of CME had been marked by a strong sense of continuity of policy, Stanier was pitched well and truly into the 'deep end'. The 'scrap and build afresh' approach he adopted was drastic, but unavoidable in the aftermath of the internal strife which had characterised the early years of the massive company. The most pressing need was on the West Coast Main Line, where a powerful, large locomotive was needed, capable of working 500-ton trains over the 401-miles route between Euston and Glasgow. The 'Royal Scot' 4-6-0s were doing good work on this route, but assisting engines were frequently needed over the gruelling climbs over Shap Fell, in Westmorland, and Beattock, north of Carlisle. The LMS was seeking to eliminate this second-engine work and Stanier's first 'Pacific' started to take shape firstly on the drawing board, and then in the enormous workshops at Crewe.

The first 'Pacific' was No. 6200 *The Princess Royal*, and whilst this pioneer was withdrawn from traffic in December 1962 and scrapped, the 'Princess Royal' class is represented today by Nos. 46201 *Princess Elizabeth* and 46203 *Princess Margaret Rose*. Stanier's first 'Pacifics' created a great deal of interest in the locomotive world of the early 1930s. What sort of machine would this GWR-trained engineer produce? Word quickly spread that the first 4-6-2 was under construction at Crewe and anticipation sharpened as the weeks passed, until No. 6200 was unveiled at Euston in June 1933, still painted in the 'works grey' finish applied to enable official photographers to obtain clear photographs. The anticipation had not been in vain, for No. 6200 was not only highly impressive, but the locomotive also provided an interesting subject for those interested in details of design.

The four cylinders (16¼in diameter x 28in stroke); driving wheels (6ft 6in diameter) and boiler pressure (250psi) were identical with those of the GWR 'King' 4-6-0: Stanier was 'playing safe' by constructing a machine of proven proportions. However, the requirement for a sustained high power output caused by the arduous nature of the Euston-Glasgow route, and the consequent voracious appetite for steam, had prompted Stanier to use a much larger boiler and firebox than that fitted to the 'King'. No. 6200 was of a completely new design, and the first example of the standard appearance which later characterised all Stanier locomotives. Stanier paid special attention to the cabs, which were roomy and comfortable for the crews, who appreciated the thoughtful layout. A second 'Pacific' followed soon after and this engine, numbered 6201 by the LMS, is the engine which survives today as BR No. 46201 *Princess Elizabeth*.

The pioneer pair were put to work between Euston and Glasgow, and whilst a good driver and fireman proved that the basic design was sound, there were initial problems with boiler performance. Detailed research carried out in 1934 prompted Stanier to redesign the boiler and the 'Princess Royal' class was expanded during 1935, when ten more engines were built of the revised design, carrying the numbers 6203-6212 and named after lady members of the British royal family. Examples were: Nos. 6205 *Princess Victoria*, 6208 *Princess Helena Victoria*, 6210 *Lady Patricia* and 6212 *Duchess of Kent*. The engines were progressively introduced onto the West Coast Main Line, working the 'Royal Scot', 'Mid Day Scot' and 'Night Scot' prestige trains on a regular basis. The satisfactory performance of the engines enabled the acceleration of the 'Mid Day Scot' in 1936 and whilst by modern standards the overall time of 7hr 35min for the Euston-Glasgow journey seems rather slow, the 59 minutes allowed for the 31.4 miles of the Carnforth-Shap summit section provided the engines and their crews with a real challenge. On this route were located the taxing climbs over the summits at Grayrigg and Shap, in the Westmorland Fells. From sea level at Carnforth, just north of Lancaster, the railway climbs to 916ft above sea level at Shap summit.

The 'Princess Royal' 4-6-2s performed well over the Anglo-Scottish main line and following the LNER's introduction of the 'Silver Jubilee' and the streamlined 'A4' 'Pacifics' in September 1935, the LMS had been sharply aware of the need to maintain its forward progress and development of train services. In late 1936 the company decided to experiment with the prospect of yet faster express running for the Coronation year of 1937. In the weeks which followed, *Princess Elizabeth* established new records for speed and power output and earned an important place in railway history. At this time, the 4-6-2 had completed 77,000 miles in service since the last General Repair at Crewe works and was coupled to one of the new Stanier 4,000 gallon tenders, of nine tons coal capacity. The trial trains were to run non-stop between Euston and

Above: An image of harnessed power at Steamtown, Carnforth as No. 6201 *Princess Elizabeth* flexes her muscles on the Museum's internal demonstration line.
John Shuttleworth.

Glasgow, and return, on November 16/17, to assess the problems and practicalities of continuous high speed running. The trial was a triumph, No. 6201 hauling the 240-tons train over the 802.8 mile journey at an overall average speed of 69mph, an achievement for continuous high speed travel with steam traction which remains unbroken today. *Princess Elizabeth* ran the $401\frac{1}{4}$ miles on the south bound journey start-to-stop in $344\frac{3}{4}$ minutes. The team spirit showed by the operating department, especially the hundreds of signalmen, who kept the busy main line clear for this amazing run, is as worthy of commendation as the skills showed by the footplatemen.

After 1948, the new British Railways regime added 40,000 to all LMS engine numbers, *Princess Elizabeth* becoming No. 46201. Superseded on the fastest and heaviest Anglo-Scottish turns after 1937 by Stanier's more powerful 'Princess Coronation' 4-6-2s, the 'Princess Royal' class continued to handle much front-line express work from London to Manchester, Liverpool and Glasgow. No. 46201 was withdrawn from Carlisle Kingmoor motive power depot in October 1962, and was privately purchased for preservation by the Princess Elizabeth Locomotive Society, which maintains the engine in main line running order, in LMS red livery. In its 29-year working life, *Princess Elizabeth* covered 1,526,807 miles in revenue-earning service. The locomotive appeared at the Rainhill celebrations of 1980 and whilst normally based at the Bulmer Railway Centre, Hereford, the engine periodically moves around the country as part of its programme of main line excursion work.

The other preserved member of the class, BR No. 46203 *Princess Margaret Rose*, is cared for as

a static exhibit at the Midland Railway Centre, Butterley, near Derby, painted in BR lined Brunswick green livery. This locomotive, one of the ten engines of this class built in 1935, was withdrawn from Carlisle Upperby MPD in October 1962, after completing 1,494,484 miles in traffic, and was purchased for preservation by Butlins Ltd. After being restored to LMS red livery at Crewe works the locomotive was placed on static display at the company's Pwllheli holiday camp. *Princess Margaret Rose* was subsequently moved to Butterley in October 1974,, where in 1985 the engine was repainted in the BR green livery in which the 'Pacific' was painted by BR after 1952. In 1987 Butlin's decided to sell their engines and the Midland Railway Centre launched an appeal to raise the £60,000 price carried by *Princess Margaret Rose*.

By 1934, the LMS also had urgent need of a fast, class 5 4-6-0 for other express passenger traffic. Stanier's answer was the three-cylinder 'Jubilee' 4-6-0, introduced in May 1934, whose basic proportions were derived from the Fowler 'Baby Scot' of 1930, none of which survive. Introduced in May 1934, the three-cylinder 'Jubilees' were not an initial success. They were afflicted by inadequate superheating and suffered from poor draughting of the fire: the result was an indifferent locomotive which in skilled hands performed barely adequately, but which otherwise quickly ran short of steam. Maintaining a locomotive in running order in the 1980s is a very expensive business and for main line operation the mandatory seven year boiler overhaul and mechanical repairs can cost around £50,000. It is therefore of interest to note in passing that, when first built, the initial batch of 50 engines (complete with tenders) cost £286,000 — just £5,720 each! A total of 191 examples of this class were built by 1936. The original batch of 113 locomotives were built and introduced into service 'straight off the drawing board' — there was no trial period with a prototype — and the first engine to be named was No. 5552 *Silver Jubilee*, in April 1935, after which the class became officially known as 'Jubilees'. By 1938, all 191 engines were named, after Dominions of the colonies and their provinces, crown colonies, naval battles and famous admirals, famous ships of the Royal Navy, pioneer engines (formerly carried by the 'Royal Scot' class, from which they had been removed in favour of more regimental names) and the counties of Ireland. The 'Jubilees thereby carried names which struck a chord with all patriotic Englishmen: *North West Frontier, Bihar and Orissa, British Guiana, British Honduras, Howe, Collinwood, Blake, Hood, Jellicoe, Jutland, Trafalgar, Achilles, Thunderer, Implacable, Revenge, Dauntless, Repulse, Warspite, Sanspareil, Comet, Phoenix* and *Samson*. Through the 1930s, a programme of improvements to boiler design and draughting arrangements developed the capabilities of the 'Jubilees' and by 1940 they were the fast, able 4-6-0s Stanier had envisaged. The class worked on fast passenger turns over all parts of the LMS network until the early 1960s, and also in parts of the Western Region, after which, as a result of large scale introductions of new diesel locomotives, they were progressively and increasingly relegated to a variety of secondary turns, including, in some instances, freight workings. On the former LMS system, the class had worked most commonly on the Midland main line from London St Pancras to Leeds, Carlisle and Glasgow, the West Coast Main Line from Euston to Wolverhampton, Liverpool, Manchester, Carlisle and Glasgow, whilst together with the Eastern and Western Regions the class operated the Bristol-Birmingham-Sheffield-Newcastle route.

By January 1957 only one of the 191 'Jubilees' had been scrapped, BR No. 45637 *Windward Islands*, which was damaged beyond repair in the appalling multiple crash at Harrow and Wealdstone, in October 1952. Planned scrapping of the class started in 1960, with the first mass withdrawals occurring in 1962. As the 1960s progressed the 'Jubilees' faded rapidly from the scene in which they had once played such a vital role: in 1964 a further 66 members of the class were scrapped, then 33 more were withdrawn in 1965 and a further seven were scrapped in 1966, leaving just eight survivors working on into 1967, their last year of everyday service. The last few survivors were gathered at Leeds Holbeck engine shed from where, to the last, they worked express services regularly over the arduous Settle-Carlisle line across the Pennines. They attracted much attention in these last days from railway enthusiasts and photographers, the last engines remaining in traffic being Nos. 45562 *Alberta*, 45593 *Kolhapur* and 45697 *Achilles*. With the summer over, *Achilles* was withdrawn in September 1967, and was subsequently cut up for scrap by Cashmore's yard, at Great Bridge, in May 1968. No. 45593 *Kolhapur* was withdrawn in October 1967 and purchased for preservation, whilst the last 'Jubilee' to remain in service was No. 45562 *Alberta*. This engine was finally withdrawn in November 1967 and was also scrapped by the Cashmore yard, at Great Bridge, in May 1968.

Of the other two preserved 'Jubilees', No. 45596 *Bahamas* is unusual in that it is fitted with a double chimney of distinctive appearance. Built in 1935, also by the NBL Company, *Bahamas* worked until withdrawal from Stockport shed, in August 1966, as BR No. 45596. Following purchase for preservation by the Bahamas Locomotive Society Ltd., No. 45596 was completely overhauled at the Leeds works of the Hunslet Engine Co. Ltd., and painted in LMS red livery as No. 5596. The 'Jubilee' has since been based at the Dinting Railway Centre, near Manchester.

Right: LMS 'Jubilee' No. 5690 *Leander* stands quietly inside the BR locomotive shed at Northwich on April 19 1982, as part of its intinerary of main line excursion work. The small '5XP' lettering beneath the cab windows denotes that No. 5690 was classified by the LMS as having a power rating classification of 5, for express passenger duties. *Leander* is normally based on the Severn Valley Railway. *Brian Dobbs.*

The best-known 'Jubilee' of the 1980s is No. 5690 *Leander*, based on the Severn Valley Railway, in the West Midlands. Built in March 1936 at Crewe, at a cost of £6,400 (including tender) No. 5690 spent much of its working life based at Bristol's Barrow Road engine shed, where it was withdrawn in March 1964, after 28 years at work. The locomotive was sold to Woodham's, of Barry, for scrap and spent the next nine years languishing in the dock sidings. In 1972, *Leander* was privately purchased for preservation and was overhauled at the BR workshops at Derby. Since 1973 the locomotive has been a familiar and popular sight on main line railtours, spending time at both the Dinting Railway Centre and the Steamtown Railway Museum, Carnforth. In 1980 *Leander* was the subject of a major overhaul at the Bridgnorth workshops of the Severn Valley Railway, which subsequently purchased the locomotive.

Stanier's finest creation and certainly the best-loved of his designs, amongst both footplate crews and lineside obsevers were his four-cylinder 'Princess Coronation' class 'Pacifics', known affectionately and most popularly as 'Duchesses'. The November 1936 runs by No. 6201 *Princess Elizabeth* had shown that a 6hr schedule was possible, but it was felt that a re-examination of the 'Pacific' design would produce a locomotive better-equipped for sustained high-speed running. Stanier departed to India as a part of an investigative team looking at the riding qualities of that country's 'Pacific' locomotives, leaving Chief Draughtsman Coleman and his team to turn the overall concept into a triumph of power and design. Whilst the engines which followed were rightly attributed to Stanier, Coleman's important role in the design should not pass without credit.

The first engine of the new class, No. 6220 *Coronation* caused a sensation when it was ceremonially rolled out of the Crewe works paintshop on May 25 1937. The Swindon influence clearly evident in the 'Princess Royal' and 'Jubilee' locomotives was gone and Stanier, now wholly familiar with the demands of LMS front line requirements, had produced a masterpiece. His former interest in moderate superheating was gone and the new engines had a very large superheating surface of 856sq ft. The 6ft 6in driving wheel diameter of the 'Princess Royal' was enlarged to 6ft 9in for the new class and the massive locomotives were more than 73ft long — but it was the appearance of the new design which caught the attention of press and public alike.

Following Gresley's introduction of the 'A4' class 'Pacific' in 1935, the streamlining craze had 'snowballed', and No. 6220 *Coronation* was therefore clothed in a wind-tunnel tested streamlined casing, with a bullet-shaped front quite different to the wedge-shaped nose of the LNER 'A4'. Painted in a striking blue livery, the locomotive carried a series of four silver stripes starting at a point above the front drawhook and sweeping upwards around the curved plating and down the sleek sides of Stanier's superb locomotive. These stripes were continued down the sides of the 'Coronation Scot' train to create an overall impression of speed and power. Even the headlamps provided for the locomotive were winged, to emphasise speed! The first five locomotives were painted in this blue and silver livery, with the second batch of five engines being painted in red, with gold trim.

The atmosphere in early 1937 must have been one of intense anticipation. Picture the scene: on the LNER, expresses hauled by Gresley's 'A4' and 'A3' class 'Pacifics' were capturing much public attention, and the British speed record for steam traction of 113 mph was credited to streamlined LNER 'A4' No. 2512 *Silver Fox*. The high-speed running recorded by No. 6201 in November 1936, and the possibility of a six-hour schedule between Euston and Glasgow was

Below: An impressive view of one of Stanier's 'Princess Coronation' class 'Pacifics' of 1937 in original streamlined condition. This is No. 6221 Queen Elizabeth, climbing past Shap Wells, in Westmorland during 1937, with a northbound express. The locomotive was painted blue, with silver stripes. BBC Hulton Picture Library.

Above: With the National Railway Museum's LNWR former Royal Train brake coach behind the tender, LMS 'Princess Coronation' 4-6-2 No. 46229 *Duchess of Hamilton* climbs Giggleswick bank, near Settle, en-route to Carnforth with a special working of April 10 1982. Although Gresley's 'A4' class holds the world speed record for steam traction, the 'Princess Coronations' were immensely powerful machines; for example, No. 46225 *Duchess of Gloucester*, whilst hauling a 900-ton simulated load on the arduous 'Long Drag' from Kirkby Stephen to Ais Gill achieved a continuous 30mph — the longest sustained power output ever recorded by a British steam locomotive. *Dave Dyson.*

causing much excitement in the LMS camp, especially after No. 6220 *Coronation* had been unveiled. Here indeed was a machine to make the LNER sit up and take notice! There was thus a degree of disappointment on the LMS when it was announced that the schedule was to be 6½ hrs, especially since the East Coast King's Cross-Edinburgh time was an even 6 hrs. However, the LMS route was less suitable for sustained high speed running than the east Coast route and in any case, the LMS route was nine miles longer than the LNER main line, and even the 6½ hr schedule necessitated faster running than ever before over some tough sections.

LMS devotees were not disappointed. After a period of running in, when it was reported that No. 6220 had recorded 95mph on level track with more than 300 tons coupled to the tender, it was announced that a press special would run from Euston, with the new engine in charge, on June 29 1937. Speculation increased that an attempt was to be made on the British speed record, then held by the LNER, and excitement increased. The press special left Euston with eight coaches behind the tender, weighing 270 tons, with Driver T.J. Clarke on the regulator. The first part of the journey, from Euston, produced some spirited running, but no determined attempt at very fast running, but on the 10½-mile descent from Whitmore to Crewe the streamlined locomotive was spurred to 114mph, thus earning for the LMS the British speed record, by a margin of just 1mph, from the rival LNER company! The feeling was that even higher speeds of up to 120mph could have been achieved, but with speed into 'three figures' and still increasing and Crewe less than two miles ahead, a very harsh brake application was needed to avoid mishap. As it was, the train lurched alarmingly as it travelled at high speed over the crossovers and complex trackwork on the approach to Crewe station, giving the passengers a very rough ride and smashing much crockery in the dining car! The 10½ miles from Whitmore had been covered at an *average* speed of more than 90mph and in reality it was a miracle (or more accurately, a tribute to both the design of the locomotive and the superb quality of the track) that the train did not derail in a horrific manner. However, No. 6220 and her train were unscathed and returned to London later in the day, at an average speed of 80mph! The 'Coronation Scot' thus went into service in a blaze of publicity for the LMS with which Stanier and Board of Directors were well pleased.

In service the new 'Pacifics' were very successful, hauling their nine-coach loads on the 6½ hr schedule between Euston and Glasgow at an average speed of just over 63mph. Sparkling performances were recorded with pleasing frequency, illustrating the soundness of the work put in by Stanier, Coleman and the team of LMS draughtsmen. However, the storm clouds were gathering over Europe, and the outbreak of war with Germany on September 3 1939 ended steam's 'golden years' in Great Britain. The unique combination of superb design, superb track, dedicated staff, careful maintenance and sharp competition never again achieved the fine-tuning and balance experienced and utilised to such good effect by the 'Big Four' companies during this marvellous period: were it not for the outbreak of hostilities, who knows what might have been achieved. As it was, the railway companies played an important part in the war years, in which time track, stock and locomotives became worn out, and in the post-war years the inevitability of Nationalisation and the problems and policies which followed ensured that never again would steam traction develop in the exciting fashion of the 1930s. With the outbreak of war, all express services were restricted to 60mph, and whilst this was subsequently relaxed to 75mph — the 'Princess Coronations', and all other express classes, had been tightly reined.

The best known of the preserved members of this class, BR No. 46229 *Duchess of Hamilton*, preserved in BR red livery and maintained in running order by the Friends of the National Railway Museum, has a particularly interesting past. In 1937 the LMS had decided that it would exhibit a complete train at the 1939 World Fair, to be held in New York, and the engine selected for display was No. 6229 *Duchess of Hamilton*. This engine therefore changed identities with pioneer No. 6220 *Coronation* and was shipped to the United States of America aboard the SS *Belpamela* with its train. Thus disguised as No. 6220 *Coronation*, No. 6229 toured the USA from March 21 to April 14 1939, after which the train was shown at the World Fair. The LMS locomotive and train were in New York when war broke out and the train remained in America until 1945, when the war ended, but the LMS had dire need of motive power and No. 6229 was shipped quietly home in 1943 to return to work and resume its own identity.

By 1947, 38 'Princess Coronation' 'Pacifics' had been built, in slightly different forms. Of the engines built by Stanier, Nos. 6220-29 and 6235-48 were all streamlined in either blue, red or (during the war) black liveries, whilst Nos. 6230-34 were built unstreamlined. The plain black livery applied to the last batch of streamlined engines (Nos. 6245-48) had been distinctly unflattering and the final batch of Stanier engines constructed, Nos. 6249-55 were also built unstreamlined. The final two engines, Nos. 6256/57, were built in unstreamlined condition under Stanier's successor as CME, H. G. Ivatt, with a number of detail differences.

The smooth, sleek casings of the early engines generated much publicity but there was a cost in terms of accessibility for maintenance, and in 1946 removal of the streamlining commenced, giving the engines a more conventional appearance. No. 46229 *Duchess of Hamilton*, built as a red and gold-liveried streamlined engine in 1938, was painted black in 1945 prior to being de-streamlined and fitted with smoke deflectors in December 1947, on the eve of Nationalisation on January 1 1948. In the late 1950s, the London Midland region of British Railways resurrrected LMS red for some of its front-line motive power and *Duchess of Hamilton* appeared in this livery in 1958. The locomotive was withdrawn in February 1964 after running more than 1½ million miles in revenue-earning service.

More new 'Pacific' classes were introduced in Britain in the 1940s. On the LNER, Gresley had died suddenly, not yet 65 years old, 'in harness' in 1941, after nearly 30 years as Chief Mechanical Engineer of the GNR/LNER, leaving Edward Thompson, then 60 years of age, to take the reins as CME — and he was not an unquestioning follower of Gresley's ideas. He was especially critical of Gresley's valve gear arrangements for the centre cylinder of three-cylinder engines, which although prone to give trouble when run-down and in need of repair, worked well when maintenance was good. For whatever reason, and every possible option from bitterness to genuine belief have been espoused as the Thompson's motivating force, the new CME set out with purpose to move as far away from Gresley's principles as he could. Thompson first rebuilt Gresley's six 'P2' class 2-8-2s as 'A2' class 'Pacifics' and then, with insulting choice of engine it has been said, rebuilt Gresley's pioneer 'Pacific' *Great Northern*, to suit his own design criteria, producing a locomotive of great ugliness. Fortunately for the memory of Gresley, Thompson was in turn succeeded in July 1946 as CME by A.H. Peppercorn, who once again produced 'Pacifics' of elegance and ability for the LNER at Doncaster. Nationalisation was on the horizon, but there was sufficient time for Peppercorn to re-work the Thompson 'A2' into a rather better design, by incorporating some of the Gresley tradition. As a consequence, 15 of the Peppercorn 'A2' class and 49 of the then-new 'A1' 4-6-2s followed.

The sole survivor of this period of LNER locomotive history is three-cylinder 'A2/3' class 'Pacific' No. 60532 *Blue Peter*, started by the LNER, but actually completed after Nationalisation as the first locomotive to emerge from Doncaster works as a British Railways locomotive. As such, the locomotive only ever carried a BR number, though since preservation the engine has been painted in LNER apple green livery as No. 532. Originally introduced by Thompson in 1943, the 'A2' class 'Pacifics' were improved and developed by Peppercorn to produce a machine of power and capability which was used to good effect on all parts of the East Coast Main Line from King's Cross to Aberdeen. Whilst the engines worked well enough, they never aspired to the heights and triumphs of the Gresley 'A4s' and Stanier 'Princess Coronations.' From the operating department's point of view however, the Peppercorn 'Pacifics' were reliable and gave much trouble-free service.

No. 60532 *Blue Peter*, named after the Derby winner of 1939, was withdrawn from service at Dundee in 1966 and was privately purchased for preservation. Scrapping of the class had started in 1962 and *Blue Peter* was the last survivor in everyday service. In recent years the locomotive has been based at the Dinting Railway Centre, where it has been steamed occasionally to give brake van rides on the Centre's short demonstration line of a few hundred yards length. However, there had been a consistent demand for this engine to return to main line railtour service and in early 1987 the locomotive owner reached agreement with the North Eastern Locomotive Preservation Group to achieve this aim.

However, there was one final chapter in the story of pre-Nationalisation express steam traction, and this was written on the Southern Railway, following the appointment in 1937 of the enigmatic O.V.S. Bulleid, formerly Gresley's assistant on the LNER, as Chief Mechanical Engineer at Waterloo. Bulleid, a designer of sharply enquiring mind and an innovative, adventurous nature, was never afraid to experiment with the unconventional, and by turning accepted practice 'on its head' produced a pair of express passenger classes (together with a freight class, examined in chapter 5) which caused much controversy and argument which continues to this day — his celebrated 'Merchant Navy' and 'West Country' class 'Pacifics' many examples of which survive in the 1980s, as listed in Chapter 9. Some are regularly steamed and haul passenger trains, both on BR main lines and at private railways, whilst others are still undergoing lengthy and expensive restoration from scrapyard condition.

Oliver Vaughan Snell Bulleid, born in 1882 in New Zealand, started his railway career in 1901, when he was apprenticed to H.A. Ivatt, CME of the GNR, at Doncaster. He rose quickly through the ranks and by 1906 he was the Personal Assistant to the Works Manager at Doncaster, but after seven years with the GNR he grew eager for change and spent some time working in France; he eventually returned to Doncaster in 1912 as Personal Assistant to H.N. Gresley, who had succeeded Ivatt as CME. Bulleid served in the Army as a railway engineer during the First World War, and after demobilisation in 1919 returned to Doncaster yet again, as Manager of the Carriage & Wagon Works. Following the Grouping of 1923 Bulleid served as Principal Assistant to Gresley who had been appointed CME of the newly-formed LNER. Gresley therefore had the quick-thinking and innovative Bulleid at his side throughout the conception, construction and fine-tuning of his finest creations, the 'A3' and 'A4' class 'Pacifics', and the detailed extent of Bulleid's contribution will never be fully known. Suffice to say that the pair made a formidable and successful team, the commanding and more cautious, though highly experienced approach of Gresley, who nevertheless recognised a good, if completely fresh idea when he saw one, and Bulleid, a highly original thinker, who in mapping out the broad scope of a new approach, perhaps overlooked some of their more practical difficulties. Gresley's mature, but enlightened

Below: Standing on the turntable at the Didcot Railway Centre on May 29 1985 is LNER 'A2' class 'Pacific' No. 532 *Blue Peter*. The 1948-built 'Pacific' was visiting Didcot at this time as part of the celebrations held that year to commemorate the 150th anniversary of the GWR. *Blue Peter* is now on loan to the North Eastern Locomotive Preservation Group, based on the North Yorkshire Moors Railway. Fitted with 6ft 2in diameter driving wheels, the 'A2' class never aspired to the successes of Gresley's 'A3' and 'A4' class 'Pacifics.' *Mike Esau.*

approach allowed him to give Bulleid every encouragement in keeping abreast of new developments and generating new ideas, which the CME sifted, keeping the good and practical proposals, and rejecting the impractical and unsound suggestions. Bulleid was kept on a tight rein under Gresley.

Like Stanier before him on the GWR, Bulleid was happy in his work and was astonished when the SR hierachy made it known to him in 1937 that the CME's office at Waterloo was his for the asking. He was 54 years old, though youthful in spirit and outlook, and had not considered leaving the LNER: he had satisfied his professional restlessness in the years before and during the First World War and was settled in his working relationship with Gresley. The SR however needed a CME of skill and experience to succeed Maunsell, who was not in the best of health and wished to retire. Bulleid applied for the post and started work at Waterloo on September 20 1937, allowing Maunsell only one month to 'show him the ropes' before he retired, leaving Bulleid in absolute command of his new empire. Bulleid certainly had drive and ambition to put his new ideas into action, but on that September morning in 1937 even he could not possibly have forseen what lay ahead in the next two decades. More to the point, the SR Board, who generally viewed the CME's task as simply obtaining the best from steam traction on the contracting non-electrified network of main lines, were due for a profound shock!

The first engines to appear during 1938, Bulleid's first year as CME, were Maunsell's 'Q' class 0-6-0 freight engines, otherwise, Maunsell's building programme had ground to a halt, partly because of his failing health after 1934 and partly because of the vociferous pro-electrification

Right: 'Merchant Navy' 4-6-2 No. 35029 *Ellerman Lines*, sectioned for display at the National Railway Museum, to show visitors the inner workings of a main line express steam locomotive. *John Coiley.*

Below: Sister locomotive No. 35028 *Clan Line* passes Fosse Road, returning from Stratford to Marylebone with 'The Shakespeare limited' of October 19 1986. *John S. Whiteley.*

lobby. No new engines had been built in 1937, for example. Consequently, whatever his zeal to 'get cracking' on a programme of new construction, as the 'new boy' Bulleid had to compromise his ideals. In his early days at Waterloo his steam work, which was limited, included the fine-tuning of the Maunsell 'Lord Nelson' 4-6-0s and the 'Schools' 4-4-0s to improve their performance, but Bulleid had grand ideas for new locomotives to replace the SR fleet of advancing age. In an official report, with characteristic wit, he wrote: " If you replace half a cavalry regiment with tanks, this does not make your horses any younger." This approach was successful and Bulleid, a courteous gentleman of considerable personal charm, persuaded the rather reticent Board to approve his bold programme of new construction.

When Bulleid moved to Waterloo, he found a very different pattern of traffic to that with which he had been familiar on the LNER. The heavy freight and endless coal trains so familiar on the LNER were gone and he was faced with a railway which had a heavy commitment to commuters, ever-expanding electrification, and a good number of fast, heavy expresses, especially the Continental boat trains, for which new and powerful steam locomotives were urgently required. Maunsell had drawn up a sketchy proposal for a 'Pacific' of his own as long ago as 1933, but as new construction generally was falling by the wayside, this ambitious project had not progressed beyond a vague proposal. Bulleid's first inclination was to build a 2-8-2, but the SR Civil Engineer prohibited the idea: the CME was thus left with the 'Pacific' wheel arrangement, and as 1939 proceeded and war approached, design work went ahead. In the CME's drawing office life was volatile, for Bulleid played a far greater role in detailed design than was normal for British CMEs. His lively approach and inventive nature caused frequent changes of plan and Bulleid spent much time discussing detailed points of design with his draughtsmen, which was unusual, and he commanded much loyalty amongst his staff.

War broke out with Germany on September 3 1939 and work on the 'Merchant Navy' (which was now on the drawing board) proceeded, though Bulleid was at one stage called to account by the Ministry of Labour, who had been informed that the SR was wasting valuable resources by building 'de-luxe' locomotives, when tank or heavy freight engines were required. The charismatic Bulleid convinced the Government that his 'Merchant Navy' class engines would be of mixed traffic capability and Ministry approval followed. With the construction of the 'Merchant Navy' class, Bulleid's adventurous and experimental nature was finally given full and free rein and he did not waste the opportunity. When the first engine, No. 21C1, appeared, it featured a host of new ideas and was revolutionary in appearance and concept from its wheels and valve gear to its boiler and capability. The heart of any steam locomotive is its boiler and the 'MN' boiler was probably the best steam generator ever fitted to a British locomotive. It was of huge capacity and for the first time in this country featured an all-steel welded firebox, designed to successfully burn coal of indifferent quality. On the road and on scientific test, the Bulleid boiler always acquitted itself with spectacular success. It was in other aspects of the 'MN' design that Bulleid's work created much heated debate and controversy, resulting in highly polarised opinions which are debated with passion even to this day. The 'Merchant Navy' class engines were all rebuilt by BR in the late 1950s along conventional lines, and it is thus impossible to see one in original condition today. However, whilst the later 'West Country' and 'Battle of Britain' class engines of 1945 were smaller than their predecessors, they were similar in appearance and not all examples were subsequently rebuilt. Thus, Nos. 34092 *City of Wells*, based on the Keighley & Worth Valley Railway, and the Bluebell Railway's 34023 *Blackmore Vale* give a good indication of how the 'MN' engines first appeared, in 1941. Other preserved examples are listed in Chapter 9.

Mechanically speaking, Bulleid's first 'Pacifics' broke new ground in their use of miniaturised, chain-driven valve gear, wholly enclosed in an oil bath. Bulleid thought that the difficulties of locomotive preparation, specifically involving the lubrication of the centre connecting rod and motion should be eliminated. It was a messy business, involving the driver clambering about in the restricted space between the locomotive frames, with his oilcan. Bulleid reasoned that totally enclosing the middle connecting rod, slide bars, crosshead and miniature valve gear in a sump containing 40 gallons of oil, would both take care of the essential lubrication and protect the

Bulleid 'West Country' 4-6-2 No. 21C123 *Blackmore Vale*, in original 'air-smoothed' condition, steams purposefully towards Freshfield Halt, on the Bluebell Railway, in Sussex. *Peter Zabek.*

reciprocating parts from abrasive grit and ash from the fire and ashpan. A pump sprayed oil over the moving parts as the engine moved, and the faster it ran, the faster the 40 gallons of oil within the oilbath was circulated. In theory it was a wholly sensible idea, and Bulleid was trying to do no more than emulate the working conditions of the connecting rod and big end in a motor car engine. However, the crank axle, which passed through the oilbath and to which the connecting rod was secured, was mounted on the locomotive's main springs and needed a degree of movement both laterally and vertically. It proved impossible to maintain an efficient oil seal around this axle and the oil bath leaked copiously, causing major problems. Oil soaked upwards into the boiler lagging, occasionally catching fire with spectacular results, and it also found its way onto the wheel treads, making worse the slipping problems to which all 'Pacifics' are prone.

In appearance also, the 'MN' class engines were of revolutionary concept, being encased in a semi-streamlined covering which Bulleid chose to call 'air-smoothed'. Being flat-fronted this casing was not intended for aerodynamic purposes; Bulleid's two-fold aim was firstly to prevent exhaust smoke and steam drifting around the boiler and obscuring the drivers forward vision, and secondly to create a locomotive which could be cleaned by automatic machinery similar to modern car washing equipment, with spinning brushes. The first engine, No. 21C1, steamed for the first time in February 1941, was unveiled at Waterloo on March 10, when it was named *Channel Packet* by Lieutenant Colonel Moore-Brabazon, and while the newspapers of the day were quite understandably preoccupied with the war, the launch of *Channel Packet* attracted useful press coverage. The following nine engines of the batch were similarly named after merchant shipping companies, a highly appropriate choice for a railway company whose services had so many maritime connections, especially in wartime. To a sea-faring nation the names had a special appeal, and examples were: *Cunard White Star, Canadian Pacific, Orient Line, General Steam Navigation* and *Blue Funnel*.

As might be expected with a machine of such novel concept, there were many 'teething troubles', so Bulleid was pleased to see his engines used mainly on freight traffic for their first months at work — and this also ensured that the new engines were seen as working in the mixed traffic capacity for which they had been authorised. Subsequently however, the 'King Arthur' 4-6-0s designed by Maunsell and introduced in 1925, were struggling with heavy passenger services in the West of England, and all ten engines of the new 'MN' class were transferred to work between Exeter and Yeovil, where when all was well they mastered their 500-ton trains.

In service the 'MN' evoked mixed reactions. They displayed virtually unlimited steaming capacity, rapid acceleration with heavy trains and a significant reserve of power. Their cabs were appreciated by enginemen, for Bulleid had grouped the controls used by driver and fireman on their own sides of the cab, meaning they could work without getting in each other's way, and this had not been normal British practice. In the past, the duplicated fittings had been arranged symmetrically, on either side of the cab, causing much 'to and fro' movement by the crew in some circumstances, and Bulleid believed that this unnecessary activity could result in a signal being missed. An electric generator powered headcode lights, while extra lights above the wheels and in the cab enabled the crew to work more easily at night. Steam operated doors covering the firehole, operated by a foot treadle, enabled firemen to close the firedoors by a small movement of the foot between each shovelful of coal. In sum, the engines were powerful, steamed well, ran fast and freely, and gave the crew a high degree of relative comfort, compared with what they had been accustomed to.

On the debit side, the 'MN' class slipped badly, both from a standing start, and whilst running under high power at speed. It is not entirely fair to castigate Bulleid's 'Pacifics' for being unique in their propensity to slip, for all high powered 4-6-2s share this trait. Gresley and Stanier 'Pacifics' both suffered from the same problem to varying degrees, but Bulleid's engines had a slightly lower adhesive weight which made slipping more likely, and the leakage of lubricant from the oil bath simply made matters worse. They could perform brilliantly when everything was going well, but they could also run poorly when the new valve-gear was giving problems, or if drivers failed to appreciate the special technique needed to avoid slipping. The very high boiler pressure (280psi) and a comparatively insensitive throttle made starting away from a standing start a delicate business. The boiler pressure was subsequently lowered by 30psi, to 250psi with good results. The problems relating to the oilbath and valve gear caused the class to spend too much time out of service in the engine sheds, where too much oil was used by fitters spending too much time on the engines. Also, whilst the 'MN' 4-6-2s demonstrated a high power capability, this was at the cost of a ferocious appetite for coal: they were not cheap to run. Bulleid claimed that high power required a substantial fuel cost, but this didn't endear him to the accountants. In the view of their critics, the engines ran too few miles, burned too much coal and used too much oil.

There were however other benefits, more difficult to quantify, but impossible to ignore. That a locomotive of such power, appearance and distinction should be built at all during the dark days of the war was in itself a near-miraculous achievement, and this had a positive and highly significant effect on morale, both on and off the railway, at a time when the peril to the nation from the enemy was at its peak. The SR derived tremendous benefit from the spin-off publicity generated by the 'MN' class engines, and their powerful exploits at high speed on heavy trains after 1943, at whatever cost, was undeniably impressive. It was not the time to quibble over efficiency; there was a war to be fought. The SR Board of Directors must have been happy, for a

Facing page: Unrebuilt Bulleid 'West Country' 4-6-2 No. 34092 *City of Wells* steams over Arten Gill viaduct, amidst the splendid scenery of the Settle-Carlisle line, with a special train on August 23 1986. Note the mounds of spoil beyond the train, tipped during excavations when the line was constructed. *Mick Roberts.*

total of 20 'Merchant Navy' 4-6-2s were built between 1941 and 1945, with 10 more following them into traffic in 1948 and 1949, after Nationalisation.

By 1945, and despite the problems afflicting the 'MN' 4-6-2s, Bulleid had persuaded the SR authorities that a lighter 'Pacific' with a wider route availability than the original class was required to work all the secondary passenger traffic on the non-electrified SR network, and as a result his 'West Country' and 'Battle of Britain' classes of so-called 'light 'Pacifics' were born. By 1951, 110 of these engines had been built, in the same innovative style as the 'Merchant Navy' class, giving the SR a total of 140 'Pacifics' — nearly three times the LMS tally of 51 'Pacifics', for a railway which featured a high-degree of electric mileage and generally less-taxing top link steam passenger jobs! Bulleid was indeed a master of diplomacy and persuasion.

Built in the same innovative style as the 'MN' class engines, the 'light Pacifics' were very similar in appearance, but were fitted with a smaller boiler and weighed around nine tons less, giving a wider route availability. The class performed well on the Kent Coast expresses and the West of England passenger duties, but with so many 'Pacifics' available, they were also found regularly working two and three-coach local services, especially over former LSWR lines in Devon and Cornwall. The Southern Region at times suffered from an embarrassment of 'Pacifics' it seemed, for which it appeared difficult to find work.

With Robert Riddles, formerly one of Stanier's assistants on the LMS, in charge as CME of the new British Railways network after 1948, Bulleid's approach fell out of favour, though interestingly, he and Riddles were both seeking the same end result — a steam locomotive which was reliable, readily available and easy to prepare, service and maintain. Bulleid had chosen the path of innovation and new approach, whilst Riddles preferred a simple, but modern form of the traditional reciprocating engine. Bulleid retired and left the British scene after Nationalisation, to work in his usual distinctive manner as CME of the railways of the Irish Republic (CIE), but that is another story. Back on the SR, his 'Pacifics' continued to polarise opinions — the crews, by now well-accustomed to their ways, respected their steaming capability, speed and power, while the engine shed staff became increasingly weary with the incessant servicing, and the accountants became increasingly alarmed at the mounting cost of keeping the engines in traffic. Finally, in the late 1950s, BR acted and embarked on a rebuilding programme which involved scrapping the enclosed valve gear, in favour of conventional valve motion, and the removal of the air-smoothed casings in favour of a more conventional appearance. Approved in 1955, the rebuilding programme started in 1956 when No. 35018 British India Line (the class were

Facing page: In biting cold, No. 34092 *City of Wells* stands in the shed yard at Steamtown, Carnforth, on December 12 1981, ready to work that day's 'Golden Arrow Pullman' special train. *W.A. Sharman.*

Below: Some of Bulleid's 'West Country' and 'Battle of Britain' class 4-6-2s were rebuilt more conventionally in the 1950s, in similar style to the larger 'Merchant Navy' class engines. No. 34016 *Bodmin,* built in 'airsmoothed' condition (as illustrated opposite by No. 34092) was subsequently rebuilt as shown here, approaching Ropley, on the Mid Hants Railway, with an afternoon train on October 20 1986. *Yvonne Lorden.*

numbered 35001 — 35030 after Nationalisation) emerged from Eastleigh works in modified form, with normal valve gear, a conventionally lagged boiler and smoke deflectors flanking the now-exposed smokebox. To those who had loved the original locomotives, the 'rebuilds' were an aberration and Bulleid himself is said to have been extremely upset, and would have preferred the class to have been withdrawn and scrapped.

The whole class of 30 'MN' engines was eventually rebuilt in similar style at a cost of £7,500 per engine, as were 60 of the smaller 'light Pacifics' of the 1945 design. They were pleasingly proportioned, and partisanship aside, were very handsome engines. More to the point, the troubles which had plagued the two classes since their early days were gone. The oil leaks and troublesome cladding both disappeared and availability and economy were both brought within satisfactory limits. The engines continued to steam well, pull hard and run at very high speeds, to the very end of steam traction on the Southern Region in 1967 — but opinions were divided amongst footplate crews about the merits of the 'rebuilds,' many men preferring the 'Pacifics' in their original form. Whatever personal preferences might be found, it is a matter of record that Bulleid's 'Pacifics' performed heroic service, in both original and rebuilt forms, until withdrawal. They handled all the prestige duties of the Southern Railway, and subsequently the Southern Region, including 'The Golden Arrow', 'The Night Ferry', 'The Royal Wessex', 'The Bournemouth Belle', and 'The Atlantic Coast Express.' In their final years of service they performed well on express services from Waterloo to Weymouth and Exeter. The 'light Pacifics' of the 'West Country' and 'Battle of Britain' classes all remained in service until 1963, when the first ten withdrawals took place. By January 1967 only 36 of the original 110 locomotives survived in service and they too had gone by July of that year, when both classes became extinct. A Bulleid 'light Pacific', No. 34100 *Appledore*, was the last steam locomotive to haul the prestigious 'Golden Arrow' from London Victoria to the Channel Coast, on June 11 1961.

The Bulleid 'Pacifics' were as popular with railway enthusiasts as they were with some of their footplate crews, and the fact that a significant number of these locomotives were sold to Dai Woodham for scrap ensured that they languished in his South Wales sidings long enough for would-be locomotive owners to raise the finance needed to rescue a 4-6-2 of their own. Many enthusiasts are therefore grateful that Woodham's men were kept fully occupied in the scrapping of redundant coal wagons bought from BR — otherwise the steam locomotives would have gone into the 'melting pot' before they could be rescued. On private sites around the country, more than two dozen Bulleid 'Pacifics' from of all three classes survive either on display, in working order, or still undergoing restoration from scrapyard condition. One of the most spectacular examples is No. 35029 *Ellerman Lines*, which was sectioned for display in the main hall of the National Railway Museum, where it is a permanent exhibit. This locomotive, built in air-smoothed condition in 1949, rebuilt at Eastleigh in September 1959, was eventually withdrawn in September 1966, and consigned to Woodham's scrapyard for cutting-up. The engine was rescued in 1973 and sectioned to the NRM's specification, involving the removal of approximately 11 tons of metalwork from the right hand-side of the locomotive. The secrets of the firebox, boiler, smokebox and cylinders are all laid bare for examination by museum visitors, who can push buttons to illuminate indicator lights to identify different components. This is one of the most popular exhibits at York — and from the left-hand side the engine looks complete!

In early 1987, the only operational 'Merchant Navy' in this country was No. 35028 *Clan Line*, built in 1948 and owned by the Merchant Navy Locomotive Preservation Society. Built in 1948, *Clan Line* was one of the last of its class to be withdrawn from service, in July 1967, and was subequently purchased for preservation. It has performed regularly on BR main line excursions throughout the 1970s and 1980s and after being based for many years at the Bulmer Railway Centre, Hereford, moved to London to appear at the head of BR's Marylebone-Stratford excursions in 1986. No. 35028, which also spearheaded Southern Region's return to steam in 1986, will eventually be joined in active service, though not on the main line, by the other eight survivors, which in Spring 1987 were in varying stages of restoration. Even more 'West Country' and 'Battle of Britain' class 'Pacifics' survive, with 16 engines in the hands of preservationists by early 1987. There is ample opportunity therefore for Bulleid enthusiasts to see his 'Pacifics' in action in Britain in the 1980s, either on Museum display, undergoing restoration to working order, pulling trains on private railways or in steam on the main line. All surviving examples are listed in Chapter 9.

Bulleid's 'Pacifics' were unusual in concept, revolutionary in appearance and controversial in service, and as the survivors return to steam they will continue to be a major attraction in the steam business of today. However, following Nationalisation in 1948 and with Robert Riddles in charge as CME, the new British Railways organisation was set on a rather more traditional course. In subsequent years a further 999 main line steam locomotives, of a dozen different classes, were built for use in Britain and the survivors of this final family of steam are depicted in Chapter 8.

CHAPTER 5:
MIXED TRAFFIC LOCOMOTIVES

Whilst express passenger work was the most glamorous aspect of a railway company's activities, it was only the tip of a very large iceberg. In addition to the large-wheeled and high-stepping passenger classes, an operating department needed engines of more general purpose, which could be called upon to carry out a variety of work from passenger service of all but the highest class, to a range of secondary and goods workings. The operator wants an engine which can go anywhere and do anything, and this can only be achieved at a certain cost, for whilst the compromise locomotive will satisfactorily work most of the passenger and freight turns of average loading and weighting, there would always be the fastest passenger trains and the heaviest goods duties for which only a specialised engine would suffice. However, used properly the well-designed mixed traffic steam locomotive was indispensable to the railways of Britain, both before and after Nationalisation.

A variety of different types and classes of mixed traffic steam locomotives are still with us in the 1980s, from all four of the 'Big Four' companies of the pre-Nationalisation era, but in general they share a common factor of having six coupled driving wheels. Quite probably the most

Above: GWR 'Manor 4-6-0 No. 7819 *Hinton Manor*, painted in BR mixed traffic lined black livery and hauling a rake of BR 'blood and custard' liveried coaches, passes Foley Park on the Severn Valley Railway, on June 22 1986. *Peter J.C. Skelton.*

Right: The cleaners apply some old-fashioned elbow grease to the Brunswick green paintwork of Collett '2251' class 0-6-0 No. 3205 at Bridgnorth, Severn Valley Railway, on September 11 1982. *Chris Milner.*

famous mixed traffic engine of all, and which can still be seen today, is William Stanier's much-loved LMS 'Black 5' 4-6-0, introduced in September 1934 and eventually multiplied into a class of 842 locomotives. Other mixed traffic classes include engines of the 0-6-0T, 0-6-2T, 2-6-0 and 2-6-2 wheel arrangements. Some of the tank engine classes are covered in Chapter 7.

The mixed traffic engine started to evolve in the second half of the 19th century, when traffic was generally heavy throughout the year, but when summer 'extras' created the need fo engines which normally hauled freight traffic to take their turn at the head of passenger trains. Such engines initially took the form of 0-6-0 tender engines, and subsequent mixed traffic designs were genarally based on this wheel arrangement. In parallel with the express passenger classes, the benefits of general advances in design, such as longer travel valve gear, higher pressure boilers, and steam superheating were progressively incorporated into the mixed traffic designs until, by the 1930s locomotive classes like the LMS 'Black 5s' and the GWR 'Hall' and 'Grange' 4-6-0s evolved as excellent all-round engines which were equally capable of deputising on the fast expresses, handling secondary passenger and parcels duties, hauling main line goods trains or pottering about on branch lines.

The 0-6-0 tender engine continued to be widely used for goods haulage by many companies, but its use in a mixed traffic capacity declined in the 20th century as train speeds rose. The GWR retained the 0-6-0 type for mixed traffic purposes however, and a unique surviving example is Collett Class 2251 0-6-0 No. 3205, built in 1946 and preserved in working order. This useful, compact locomotive is interesting not least in that the GWR relied far less on the 0-6-0 tender type than the other 'Big Four' railway companies. However, by the late 1920s the GWR's traditional 'Dean Goods' 0-6-0s were of decreasing widespread use in the face of increasing train weights, and the '2251's' were constructed to take over their role on main line intermediate work, enabling the older and smaller 'Dean Goods' engines to be transferred to more suitable duties, such as on the metals of the former Cambrian Railways.

The GWR met much of its intermediate traffic requirement after 1910 with the 2-6-0 type (a wheel arrangement imported from America) of the '43xx' class designed by Churchward. Survivors in preservation are 1917-built No. 5322, based at the Didcot Railway Centre, home of the Great Western Society, and No. 9303, on the Severn Valley Railway. This class of engines, built between 1910 and 1932, were of very useful mixed traffic capability and worked over most parts of the GWR system, their wide route availability resulting from a relatively low axle loading. Didcot-based No. 5322 has a particularly interesting history, for the engine spent its first two years of life in France, assisting Britain's war effort. Completed in August 1917 at a cost of £3,312 (plus £471 for the tender) No. 5322 returned to GWR service in 1919 and was thereafter based at Wolverhampton, Chester, Weymouth, Bristol St Phillips Marsh, Oxley, Swindon, Tyseley and Pontypool Road. The engine was withdrawn in April 1964 and despatched for scrap to Barry docks, from where it was rescued as only the third engine to leave Barry for preservation, in 1969. No. 5322 was first restored to working order at Caerphilly by members of the Great Western Society, and was the first GWS engine rescued from Barry to be restored and steamed. The engine was subsequently transferred to Didcot, where it can still be seen today.

The Collett '56xx' class 0-6-2Ts, although best known for their work on the heavy coal traffic of the South Wales valleys, for which they were primarily provided, were officially designated as mixed traffic engines. In BR days some examples were consequently painted in lined green livery, in contrast to the unlined black livery normally accorded to goods engines. Introduced in 1924, the '56xx' class was an updated Collett-version of the traditional 0-6-2T locomotives of the GWR's South Wales constituents, such as the Taff Vale and Rhymney Railways.

By 1928, the GWR's Swindon workshops had built 150 examples of this class, whilst Tyneside locomotive builders Armstrong Whitworth constructed a further 50 engines under contract, for at the time Swindon works was busy building Collett's magnificent four cylinder 'Castle' 4-6-0s. The class remained intact until 1962, when the first withdrawals commenced, although the events of 1963 and 1964 illustrated the speed with which BR moved away from steam traction, when 114 engines were scrapped from this class alone. The class became extinct in 1965, but in 1987 seven of these 0-6-2Ts were safely preserved (as listed in Chapter 9). The most popular of the GWR's mixed traffic engines were the two-cylinder 'Hall', 'Grange' and 'Manor' 4-6-0s and today, examples of the 'Hall' and 'Manor' classes are still at work, but sadly, not a single 'Grange' survived the cutter's torch; all 80 examples were scrapped. Once again, it is entirely due to the

Above: BR-black liveried GWR '56xx' 0-6-2T No. 6619 works steadily past Farwath, on the North Yorkshire Moors Railway, with the 5pm service from Pickering on July 27 1985. The NYMR runs passenger trains through spectacular scenery between Grosmont and Pickering — a distance of 18 miles. *Mike Roberts.*

dedication, efforts and praiseworthy achievements of the amateur railway preservationists that any of the GWR's two-cylinder mixed traffic engines such as the 'Halls' and 'Manors' can be seen at all — not a solitary example of either class exists in the National Collection. The only example of Churchward's two-cylinder developments represented in official preservation is 1905-built class '28xx' 2-8-0 heavy freight engine No. 2818. That is not to say that official preservationists of the 1950s and 1960s were negligent, for in those two decades there was an attitude of extreme hostility towards steam traction, which was being swept from the network with ruthless speed and a good deal of waste. Tht any engines at all were officially preserved as a National Collection remains as a tangible tribute to men like John Scholes, who as Curator of Historical relics for the British transport Commission from 1951 was responsible for all forms of land transport covered by the Commission. He is best remembered for his role in establishing of the Museum of British Transport at Clapham, and the GWR Museum at Swindon.

The surviving GWR 'Hall' and 'Manor' class engines are both direct descendants of Churchward's two-cylinder 'Saint' 4-6-0s, introduced in 1905. In traffic, the two-cylinder 'Saints' could sprint almost as fast as their four-cylinder 'Star' counterparts, but they did not run quite as sweetly. They were regarded as being 'second notch' express passenger power, rather than as mixed traffic engines, for after 1911, all intermediate passenger and freight work was usually allocated to the hundreds of 2-6-0s built to Churchward's '43xx' design. However, in the post-war years, and especially the immediate post-grouping years, train speeds and loadings were increasing again and there was pressure towards 4-6-0 rather than 2-6-0 locomotives for mixed traffic duties.

Collett's team, which prominently featured William Stanier at this time, set to work with enthusiasm on a development of their sacred Churchward principles to resolve the question, and in December 1924 two-cylinder 'Saint' 4-6-0 No. 2925 *Saint Martin* was taken into Swindon works for modification. It emerged with smaller driving wheels of 6ft diameter (compared with the original 6ft 8½in wheels) and the locomotive was an immediate success in everyday traffic. *Saint Martin* was the prototype 'Hall' 4-6-0 and a planned programme of new construction of the class commenced in December 1928, with No. 4901 *Adderley Hall*, followed by an initial batch of a further 79 engines. Subsequent variations were incorporated into successive batches, and an overall total of 330 'Halls' were built, all named after country houses, resulting in names of elegance and taste nicely in tune with the image the GWR liked to project. As with the 'Castles', which were still being built by BR 30 years after they had originally been designed, the 'Hall' 4-6-0s stood the test of time, the last batch being built by BR in 1950. In 1928, No. 4901 *Adderley Hall* had cost about £5,300 to build, including the tender; by 1950, the last batch of 'Halls' cost an average of £11,107 each, also including tenders. A measure of the wasteful speed with which BR scrapped steam in the 1960s is implied by the average mileages recorded by successive batches of these locomotives. For example, the original 1928 group of 80 engines recorded average individual mileages of around 1,302,000, whereas the 1950-built engines recorded approximately 482,000 miles each before scrapping.

By 1965, only 50 'Halls' were still at work and by October of that year the last 16 survivors were based at Oxford engine shed: the class was extinct by the year-end. Preservationists rallied and in 1987 ten examples were in private hands, as detailed in Chapter 9. Nos. 5900 *Hinderton Hall* and 4930 *Hagley Hall* have both appeared at the head of main line steam specials, as well as being regularly steamed at their respctive homes at Didcot and the SVR, in the 1980s. A long-standing aim of the GWS is to rebuild Barry refugee No. 4942 *Maindy Hall* (built 1929) as a 'Saint' 4-6-0, thereby reversing the process by which *Saint Martin* was originally turned into the 'Hall' prototype in 1924.

The significance of the 'Hall' 4-6-0 was that it was the forerunner of the modern general purpose steam locomotive generally, through subsequent pre-Nationalisation mixed traffic designs of the 1930s and 1940s, to the simple but capable machines designed and built by Robert Riddles for British Railways, after 1948 (See Chapter 8). On the GWR, the 'Hall' set in motion development which produced another two general purpose two-cylinder 4-6-0s. With the 'Hall' 4-6-0s in service, the GWR found itself in need of replacing more of the ageing '43xx' 2-6-0s built by Churchward, and assisted by the standardisation implemented since Churchward's early years, the GWR produced the 'Grange' 4-6-0s by utilising basic parts of 1911-vintage 2-6-0s. No. 6801 *Aylburton Grange* was the first example to be scrapped in 1960, but the class remained in service until as late as 1965, when 45 examples were still at work. The last four 'Grange' 4-6-0s were withdrawn in December 1965, but to the intense regret of GWR enthusiasts today, none were bought for posterity. At this time, money was scarce for the amateur preservationist and official preservation had to be limited to specific engines of particular significance and it was therefore inevitable that some classes would 'slip the net'.

In January 1938 the GWR introduced yet another two-cylinder mixed traffic design, the 'Manor' class of 30 engines. They were given a relatively light axle-loading and were intended for service over secondary routes barred to the heavier 'Hall' and 'Grange' 4-6-0s already at work. Like the 'Granges' before them, the 'Manors' were produced with great economy, as conversions from '43xx' 2-6-0s which were increasingly inadequate for the demands placed upon them. The 'Manors' worked on most parts of the GWR, mainly in passenger service, and they were particularly well known in later years for their purposeful work on the 'Cambrian Coast Express', working the arduous route from Shrewsbury to Pwllheli with conspicuous success. They were to

Facing page: A delightful scene on the Severn Valley Railway, as GWR 'Hall' 4-6-0 No. 6960 *Raveningham Hall* conjures images of the country railway of yesteryear as it passes Safari Park on April 1 1986, with the 12.35pm train from Bridgnorth. *Andrew Bell.*

be found on Cambrian metals until 1965, their last year of service for BR. In 1987, nine 'Manors' were either in service on private railways, or were still undergoing restoration from scrapyard condition following purchase from Dai Woodham, in South Wales (See Chapter 9).

It is of interest and significance to note that the 'Hall' 4-6-0s were conceived, built and successfully put to work shortly before William Stanier, Chief assistant to Collett, left Swindon in 1932 to take up his new appointment as Chief Mechnical Engineer of the LMS, where within two years he introduced the two-cylinder 'Black 5' 4-6-0, the most successful and numerous mixed traffic engine ever built. They were known on the railway as 'the engineman's friend'. When Stanier started work in January 1932, the LMS had by no means recovered from the factional dispute of its early years and there was a desperate need for a general purpose engine of class 5 capability. No existing class was suitable for large-scale multiplication as a standard design: the Hughes-Fowler 'Crab' 2-6-0, a class 5 mixed traffic engine of 2-6-0 wheel configuration, was assessed for this vital role, but was judged unsuitable. The 'Crab' was a very capable engine, its 'nickname' resulting from the appearance of their noticeably inclined cylinders, elevated running plate and distinctive motion. They were designed by George Hughes, the last CME of the Lancashire & Yorkhire Railway prior to the Grouping of 1923, and first CME of the LMS, until 1925, and subsequently built under the direction of his successor, Sir Henry Fowler. Provided to meet an urgent need from early 1920s for a locomotive capable of handling fast goods trains and intermediate passenger services, the 'Crabs' were a useful addition to the motive power fleet of the early LMS. They were capable of hauling passenger trains at speeds of up to 75mph as well as 'slogging' away powerfully with heavy freight workings. Two 'Crab' 2-6-0s are preserved BR No. 42700 in the National Railway Museum and No. 42765 on the Keighley & Worth Valley Railway.

Stanier's first locomotive design was a class of 40 mixed traffic 2-6-0s, introduced in 1933, of which a solitary example, BR No. 42968, is based on the Severn Valley Railway. Withdrawn in December 1966, this engine was rescued from Barry in December 1973 and in 1987 was approaching the final stages of a restoration to working order of around 15 years duration —

railway preservation is not for the impatient or faint-hearted! These mixed traffic 2-6-0s were in essence a smaller version of the magnificent 'Black 5' 4-6-0 mixed traffic engine introduced in September 1934, less than four months after the 'Jubilee' class 5 express passenger engines, described in Chapter 4. In outward appearance, the 'Black 5' was very similar to the 'Jubilee' 4-6-0, but in inspiration and even its basic proportions, the new Stanier class was based on the 'Hall' 4-6-0 of the GWR. However, Stanier combined the best of GWR practice with his own ideas and developments to make the 'Black 5' into a most successful and well-liked general purpose engine. They were easy to drive and fire, straightforward and cheap to maintain, and performed

well with fast passenger or heavy freight workings. Stanier paid much attention to the cabs which were spacious, well laid-out and popular with engine crews. By 1951, when BR built the last examples, 842 were in service in many different parts of the country, and before BR's rapid and ruthless run-down of steam traction in the 1960s they were so commonon the former LMS system that many trainspotters would howl in disappointment when one of their 'regulars' appeared, whilst some lineside photographers refused to 'waste' film on them! Within ten years, they had gone.

In such a large class, it was inevitable that modifications would be incorporated into successive batches and whilst it would be foolish to wager on the popular adage that 'no two Black 5s were the same' there were certainly a great number of detail differences between different batches. Some were not so noticeable superficially, such as the provision of roller bearings, others, such as the Stephenson's link motion fitted to BR No. 44767 were very prominent, and the fortunate survival of No. 44767, now named *George Stephenson*, enables us to compare the traditional Walschaerts valve gear fitted to the majority of the class with the Stephenson equivalent. A measure of its success and influence is also revealed by the way in which Stanier's 'Black 5', thinly disguised, became the standard Class 5 4-6-0 introduced by Riddles after Nationalisation, described in Chapter 8.

In the middle and late 1960s, when steam was fighting a rearguard action, the simplicity of the 'Black 5' stood it in very good stead. As maintenance schedules became unhinged and were finally abandoned altogether as the end approached, the 'Black 5' soldiered on, frequently wheezing steam from every joint, unkempt and filthy, and usually with a tender full of slack and slurry, but still roaring away, pulling trains of all types. It was fitting that they should be active to the very end of everyday steam in August 1968, when in addition to running back and forth between the Yorkshire coalfields and the Lancashire power stations, they provided some

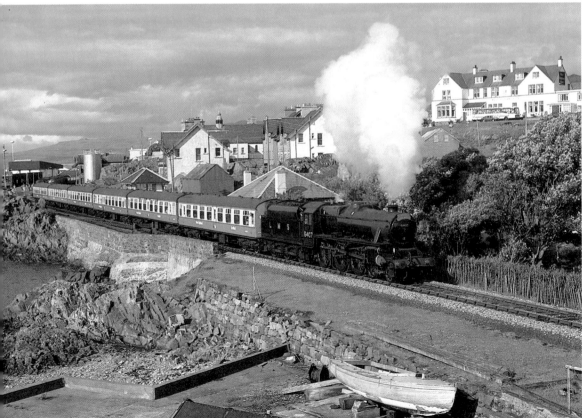

Above: Steam in silhouette. On December 6 1986 Stanier 'Black 5' No. 44932 passes Butterley reservoir, at the Midland Railway Centre, near Derby, whilst at work with Santa Special duties. For the imaginative photographer, steam locomotives offer many opportunities. *Tom Heavyside.*

Left: One of the most successful new programmes of steam excursions inaugurated in the 1980s were those over the West Highland line, from Fort William to the fishing port of Mallaig. Here we see Stanier 'Black 5' No. 5407, in the black livery applied by the LMS to its mixed traffic engines, leaving Mallaig with the 6pm departure for Fort William. *W.A. Sharman.*

Above: You can almost feel the cold! Ivatt mixed traffic 2-6-0 No. 43106 is prepared at Bewdley for Santa Special duties on the Severn Valley Railway, on December 12 1981. This view clearly shows the high running plate, giving unrestricted access to the wheels and motion, a design feature which was later incorporated on the BR Standard range of locomotives introduced after 1948. *Peter J.C. Skelton.*

sparkling eleventh-hour performances on the Preston-Liverpool passenger trains, with the steam enthusiast crews of Lostock Hall engine shed putting up a defiant last stand. A Stanier 'Black 5', No. 44871, became the last BR steam locomotive of all to have its fire drawn, in August 1968. Purchased for preservation, this historic 4-6-0, now named *Sovereign* is preserved.

The final design of LMS mixed traffic 2-6-0, the Ivatt class 4MT of December 1947 is represented in preservation by sole survivor No. 43106, based in main line running order on the Severn Valley Railway. No. 43106 is also significant in that it is a representative of the last new LMS design introduced before Nationalisation, which took place less than a month after this class was introduced. Ivatt's design previewed many features which became common with the introduction by BR of the Riddles standard engines, after 1948; for example, a high running plate to facilitate access to the wheels and motion for preparation, cleaning and repair, and a narrow coal bunker to give a clear view from the cab when running tender first. Notwithstanding this approach, Ivatt's class 4 2-6-0s did not achieve the same pleasing appearance as the Riddles engines, and were known to railwaymen as 'Doodlebugs' and to enthusiasts as 'Flying Pigs' or 'Flying Bedsteads', because of their ungainly appearance.

In contrast with the heavily industrialised nature of much of the LMS territory, the Southern Railway was very much a passenger-carrying system, dealing with enormous numbers of commuters each day, particularly around London. Other major traffic included the heavy continental boat trains, trans-Atlantic boat train connections to Southampton docks, huge numbers of summer 'extras' and a network of local passenger routes. The SR's requirement for a substantial number of mixed traffic types was perhaps rather less than those of the GWR and LMS, but the SR had its share, some of which were inherited at the Grouping of 1923 from three major constituent companies, the London & South Western Railway, the London Brighton & South Coast Railway, the South Eastern & Chatham Railway.

Despite the SR's very heavy commitment to passenger work, there was a considerable amount

Left: A striking and evocative view at Bridgnorth,
on the Severn Valley railway, as Ivatt class 4MT
2-6-0 No. 43106 (furthest
from the camera) and
class 2MT 2-6-0 No. 46521
prepare to depart from
Bridgnorth on December
9 1984. *Colin Binch.*

of freight traffic on some routes, and in March 1920, LSWR Chief Mechanical Engineer Robert W.
Urie introduced his two-cylinder 'S15' class 4-6-0, a direct development of the 'N15' 4-6-0, from
which the Maunsell 'King Arthur' 4-6-0s of 1925 were also derived (See also Chapter 4). The
class of 20 'S15s' were used primarily to haul express goods trains from Feltham yard but they
were also used at speeds of up to 70mph on passenger workings at peak times, and they
eventually ran in all parts of the SR system. They did not score highly in thermal efficiency
ratings, but their massive mainframe construction and solidly built boilers and machinery
produced a sturdy, reliable engine which could be worked very hard at minimal repair cost. They
might have burned more coal than perhaps they ought to have done but in many ways, they were
an ideal engine for the operating department.

The Mid Hants Railway, home of preserved 'S15s' Nos. 30499 and 30506, is also host to
another trio of SR-built mixed traffic locomotives with fascinating individual histories; 'U' class
2-6-0s Nos.31806 and 31625, and sole-surviving 'N' class 2-6-0 No. 31874. At the time of going to

Above: SR Class 'S15' 4-6-0 No. 841, in unlined Southern Railway black livery, leads the 11.10am Grosmont-Pickering service past Green End, North Yorkshire Moors Railway, on October 4 1986. *Andrew Bell.*

Right: In respendent condition, SR 'U' class 2-6-0 No. 31806 stands in Ropley yard, awaiting its next turn of duty on the Mid Hants Railway, on April 9 1982. No. 31806 is painted in BR mixed traffic lined black livery. *Mike Pope.*

press, Nos. 31874 and 31806 were both operational and hauling passenger trains on the MHR, painted in BR mixed traffic lined black livery.

The two-cylinder 'N' class has a particularly interesting history, as this design originated on the South Eastern & Chatham Railway, during the First World War. The demands placed on the railways of the south east at this time were particularly severe, and it became essential to run trains which were as heavy as possible, in order to keep the main lines clear. The 'N' class was intended to meet this specific requirement, though it was also designed with a mixed traffic role in mind, to facilitate seasonal use on heavy passenger trains. Distinctive in appearance, if rather austere when compared with the copper and brass-trimmed ornateness of the pre-war days, but with a capable, workmanlike air, there was much of contemporary GWR influence to be found in the more technical aspects of the two-cylinder 'N' class prototype, which was introduced in August 1917.

Between 1920 and 1922, the SECR built 15 more examples of the class, and a contemporary proposal that the 'N' should be built as a standard design led to an order being placed for 100 more engines. However, when the railways were grouped in 1923 into four large private concerns, rather than being nationalised as had been proposed at an earlier stage, construction was halted with only 50 engines completed, and these were bought by the SR. 50 of these 2-6-0s were built at Woolwich Arsenal, in a post-war scheme to relieve unemployment, and 15 more were constructed at Ashford. The MHR's No. 31874 was completed in September 1925 and worked until withdrawal in April 1964, when it was despatched to Woodham's scrapyard, at Barry. The engine was bought privately in April 1973 and transferred to the MHR, where just 2½ years later the engine was back in steam again.

Two-cylinder Maunsell 'U' class 2-6-0 No. 31806 has a rather different, although equally interesting background in that it was originally built at Brighton in 1926 as a 'K' class 2-6-4T. A contemporary design to the 'N' class 2-6-0, the 'K' class 2-6-4T was intended for fast, main line passenger work, but construction of the initial batch of 20 engines was still in progress when No. A800 *River Cray* was involved in the Sevenoaks disaster of August 24 1927, leading to a decision

Above: A beautifully recreated scene at Medstead & Four Marks station, Mid Hants Railway, on October 26 1985 as 'N' class 2-6-0 No. 31874 arrives from Alton, with a passenger service for Ropley and Alresford. Note the immaculately rebuilt signalbox, complete with fire bucket and hanging basket.
Mike Esau.

to rebuild the existing 'K' class 2-6-4Ts as 2-6-0 tender engines. There was also concern about the limited water capacity of the 2-6-4T type. Thus, the MHR 'U' class engine, BR No. 31806, started life in 1926 as 2-6-4T No. A806 *River Torridge*, before being rebuilt in its present configuration in 1928. The 'U' class locomotives were used regularly on a great deal of secondary passenger working, and they were capable of high speed, given a clear road. The 'U' class, although heavier and fitted with slightly larger driving wheels than the older 'N' class 2-6-0s, were similar in overall appearance and extremely versatile in everyday use on both passenger and freight workings. The class remained intact until 1962, after which they were steadily whittled away by withdrawals, until extinction came in 1965.

The LNER had a distinct need for mixed traffic engines, for in addition to its extensive network of express, secondary and local passenger services, there was a very heavy freight commitment. Thus, in addition to the large number of specialised freight locomotives in use on the LNER, some of which are described in Chapter 6, mixed traffic locomotives were an essential ingredient. In common with the other three pre-Nationalisation companies, six coupled driving wheels were common, and preserved general purposes engines from the LNER can be see in the 1980s in 0-6-0, 2-6-2, 4-6-0 and 2-6-0 wheel arrangements. However, the earliest LNER mixed traffic engines were of the traditional 0-6-0 wheel arrangement.

One of the oldest general purpose LNER group engines surviving in working order is North Eastern Railway 0-6-0 No. 876, classified as 'J21' by the LNER and given BR No. 65033 after 1948. Designed by T.W. Worsdell, 201 examples were built, of which 171 were constructed as two-cylinder compound engines: all were modified as simple engines before the Grouping of 1923. Used widely on both goods and passenger services, the class was introduced in September 1886. The survival of BR No. 65033 was a remarkable accident, the engine having been withdrawn from service 23 years earlier, at the outbreak of the Second World War in 1939, but reinstated within a month in view of the emergency. Originally listed for official preservation, a changed decision led to the engine being sold to a scrap dealer and cutting-up was imminent when the 0-6-0 was rescued. The 1889-built locomotive is used on the demonstration railway at Beamish, the North of England Open Air Museum.

Below: An attractive scene at the 200-acre North of England Open Air Museum, at Beamish, County Durham, on August 26 1983. This unusual Museum features a 1/4-mile working standard gauge railway and pictured here (right) is NER 0-6-0 No. 876, built in 1889, accompanied by Hawthorn Leslie 0-4-0ST No. 14, a shunting locomotive built in 1914. *Nigel Harris.*

In the 1930s the LNER inaugurated a new service of express goods traffic from the yard adjacent to its London terminus at King's Cross. The service was introduced to compete with the growing threat posed by road haulage operations and the first engine of the 'V2' class, introduced in June 1936, was named *Green Arrow* as the impressive symbol of the new registered goods facility. The 'V2' was the only tender locomotive of the 2-6-2 ('Prairie') wheel arrangement to be built in quantity for use in this country and it was indeed a successful overall design, but, like all Gresley's large three-cylinder engines, they were nevertheless subject to the difficulties caused by the conjugated valve gear during times of minimal maintenance. Inattention to lubrication caused the pins of the levers which worked the valves of the middle cylinder to become worn and the engines became very audibly 'off-beat' as a consequence. Kept in good order, this valve gear gave few problems, but it was not particularly suited to the difficult operating conditions of the war years.

Notwithstanding this, the 'V2' 2-6-2s have been described as the finest mixed traffic engines ever to run in Britain, and they are certainly a design of elegance and beauty. Modern students of the steam locomotive are fortunately able to decide for themselves, for pioneer 'V2' No. 4771 *Green Arrow* is preserved as part of the National Collection, maintained in main line running order. *Green Arrow*, the sole survivor of the 184 examples of this class built between 1936 and 1944, has in the 1980s appeared both as an important exhibit in the Main Hall of the National Railway Museum, and also in charge of passenger trains on main line routes. That the NRM successfully manages to combine the provision of an attractive museum with the aim of showing steam actually at work, working trains is worthy of praise, for neither option is either cheap or easy. It will always be impossible to please all the people, all the time, but by pursuing this dual approach the NRM provides much pleasure for thousands of general visitors and knowledgeable enthusiasts alike. The high costs of maintaining a steam locomotive to BR's demanding standards for main line operation are always escalating to new heights, and it is to be hoped that a successful formula can be found to keep this novel approach alive. It would be a sad loss to the steam scene if the working locomotives from the National Collection were to be placed on permanent static display.

Including *Green Arrow*, only eight engines were named, and two of these engines probably had the longest names ever applied to steam locomotives. These were (BR Nos): 60809 *The Snapper, The East Yorkshire Regiment, The Duke of York's Own* and 60835 *The Green Howard, Alexandra, Princess of Wales Own Yorkshire Regiment.* In passing, it is worth pointing out that the the naming of steam locomotives throughout the history of Britain's railways is an interesting subject for study in its own right, but the LNER especially had a very varied policy, which on occasions produced some bizarre names. For the 'A3s' the company chose famous racehorse

Below: A majestic sight at York, as Gresley 'V2' class 2-6-2 No. 4771 *Green Arrow* passes under the Holgate Road bridge, south of the city's impressive station, in charge of a special working for Manchester on April 26 1986. *Green Arrow* was in steam for the opening of the National Railway Museum, in September 1975, when it was driven by HRH the Duke of Edinburgh. *John Cooper-Smith.*

names, presumably in view of their high speed qualities. Thus, passengers who followed the 'sport of kings' would undoubtedly have appreciated these names, but imagine the non-racing enthusiast, strolling to the front of his LNER express and finding an 'A3' named *Brown Jack, Blink Bonny, Pretty Polly,* or *Spearmint!* Finally, in contrast to the very long name applied to 'V2' 2-6-2s Nos. 60809 and 60835, the LNER probably had the shortest name ever applied to a steam locomotive − class 5MT 'B1' 4-6-0 No. 61018 *Gnu!* The 'B1' class is decribed in more detail later in this chapter.

The 'V2' 2-6-2s worked a wide variety of fast freight and passenger services, and were popular with enginemen for their sure handling, and liked by the fitters for their reliability and ease of maintenance. The first 'V2' scrappings occurred in 1962 and by January 1964 only 69 survived: their last year of service was 1966. No. 60800 *Green Arrow* was officially preserved on withdrawal in August 1962 after which the locomotive was stored. In the early 1970s, John Scholes, then Curator of the Museum of British Transport, Clapham, approved a proposal by Bill Harvey, formerly Shedmaster at Norwich, that the engine be returned to working order. In 1973 this aim was accomplished and *Green Arrow* subsequently returned to main line excursion service.

A working example of an LNER 2-6-0, is class 'K1' 2-6-0 BR No. 62005, built in 1949 after Nationalisation, and preserved today as the sole survivor of its class, on the North Yorkshire Moors Railway. E.P. Thompson, who had succeeded Sir Nigel Gresley as CME of the LNER in 1941, had rebuilt three-cylinder 'K4' No. 61997 *MacCailin Mor* as a two-cylinder engine, thereafter designated as a 'K1/1' class 2-6-0. Thompson was in turn succeeded as CME in 1946 by A.H. Peppercorn, who slightly increased the length of the revised design to produce the 'K1' of 1949, of which 70 examples were eventually built, including No. 62005. Although of LNER origin, this locomotive was constructed as BR No. 62005 and never carried LNER livery or number at any stage of its working life. However, following withdrawal from service in December 1967 No. 62005 was preserved and painted in LNER apple green, with the notional number 2005 on the cabsides. The 2-6-0 entered passenger service on the 18-mile NYMR line between Grosmont and Pickering in June 1974 and has since made periodic forays on BR main lines with special workings.

From the regime of Edward Thompson, we can also see today two examples of the very successful 'B1' class mixed traffic 4-6-0 of 1942. These locomotives are Nos. 1306 *Mayflower*, built in 1948, and LNER No. 1264 of 1947, both based on the Great Central Railway. *Mayflower* is preserved in working order, in LNER livery, whilst No. 1264, which requires extremely extensive and costly boiler repairs, was still undergoing restoration at Loughborough in the late 1980s. More than 400 'B1s' were built for service in many parts of the LNER territory; 18 engines were named after Directors of the LNER whilst a further 40 carried the names of species of

antelope. This resulted in a very mixed bag of names, from *William Henton Carver, Harry Hinchcliffe,* and *Viscount Ridley* to *Bongo, Gazelle, Puku* and *Umseke!*

The 'B1' was hurriedly designed at a time when wartime traffic demanded a reliable, general purpose machine capable of both speed and high power. With the war at its height there was neither the will, time or finance to start producing a wholly new design, and Thompson produced a capable and very useful locomotive from existing machine tools, components and patterns already in use for other classes. Thus, the pioneer 'B1' 4-6-0 *Springbok* featured the boiler and firebox of the Gresley 'Sandringham' 4-6-0 of 1928, the cylinders of the GNR 'K2' 2-6-0 of 1914 and the wheels of the 'Green Arrow' 2-6-2 of 1936 — an ingenious and economical use of resources. Primarily designed for mixed traffic purposes, the 'B1' 4-6-0s showed a clean pair of heels with passenger trains, given a willing crew and a clear road, and they were as successful on LNER routes, both before and after Nationalisation, as Stanier's 'Black 5' 4-6-0s were on the LMS system. Both types shared roughly the same proportions, and whilst assimilating his 'B1' 4-6-0 from existing components in 1942, Thompson would have been sharply aware of the achievements of the 'Black 5' and was undoubtedly guided by its basic concept and proportions.

The quality of the 'B1' was brought into sharp focus by the locomotive interchange trials held by Robert Riddles' new team in 1948, in the course of which a 'B1' was rostered to work a GWR express on the main line between Bristol and Exeter. The engine hauled the 14-coach train of about 500-tons weight at sustained speeds of nearly 70mph — no mean achievement for a 4-6-0 of such relatively modest proportions. This sparkling performance in the early months of the new BR regime, is the logical point at which to close this brief survey of the overall growth and development of the general purpose engine, prior to Nationalisation. The phrase 'maids of all work' was never used more appropriately than in describing these remarkable engines, which could satisfy, as far as possible, the requirement by the operating departments for a genuine all-round locomotive. Frequently taken for granted during their working lives, their importance has since been brought into sharp focus. The mixed traffic classes were never as glamorous or as exciting as the crack express engines, but they nevertheless made a wonderful contribution.

Above: Thompson 'B1' class 4-6-0 No. 1306 *May-flower* and LNER 'N2 0-6-2T No. 4744 steam through the Leicester-shire landscape on October 22 1983, as they leave Loughborough, on the Great Central Railway, with a six-coach pas-senger train bound for Rothley.
John Cooper-Smith.

CHAPTER 6:
DELIVERING THE GOODS

Above: Steam in the night. 'Somerset & Dorset' '2-8-0 No. 13809 stands in the shed yard at Butterley, Midland Railway Centre, after Santa Special duties on December 22 1985.

John Cooper-Smith.

The excitement, prestige and glamour of the express passenger train and its pedigree locomotives have always been the focus of much attention for pressmen, the travelling public and the railway enthusiast alike. Top of the list have always been the evocatively named trains — the 'Atlantic Coast Express', the 'Cornish Riviera Limited', the 'Flying Scotsman' or the 'Royal Scot' for example — and where a sleek, streamlined locomotive was at the head of train, even more publicity and mystique was generated. The express passenger services of this nature have certainly been important aspects of railway history, but in accountancy terms they did not generate as much revenue as the superficially more mundane goods train. The railways were born in the service of industry, and since the days of Stephenson, Hackworth and Trevithick,

Britain's railways have needed goods locomotives of steadily increasing size and power, and in the 1980s many examples can still be seen at work.

Many of the goods locomotives still in steam today have been rescued, like many passenger engines, from amongst the abandoned hulks which occupied Dai Woodham's South Wales scrapyard from the 1960s. Years of patient fund-raising and laborious restoration have resurrected these workhorses to provide a glimpse of the powerful muscle which the railways of Britain used to such effect in helping industry to develop. Without the railways and the cheap, reliable and fast transport they provided, the rapid industrial growth of the 19th century would not have occurred, for transport had hitherto only been possible on muddy, rutted roads, or latterly canals, both dependent for power on the horse, which thereby restricted speed. With the coming of the railways in the early 19th century, industrial development was spurred from a canter into a gallop — and at the heart of it all was the steam locomotive.

The opening of the Stockton & Darlington Railway in 1825 effectively raised the curtain on Britain's railway development, although rudimentary rail-roads in the immediate vicinity of mines and quarries had been used before this date. However, the opening of the S&D as the country's first successful railway, for the transport of coal between two major centres, finally illustrated the enormous potential of this revolutionary form of transport. Stephenson's *Locomotion* had played a leading role in this exciting opening act, as did *Rocket*, five years later, at the opening of the Liverpool & Manchester Railway. Echoes of the pioneering motive power of this era can still be seen in steam today, following the construction in the 1970s of working 'replicas' of *Locomotion, Rocket* and other engines from the Rainhill trials of 1830. In this chapter we shall look briefly at how freight traffic developed on Britain's railways, and the important influence this brought to bear on the powerful locomotives developed to 'deliver the goods.'

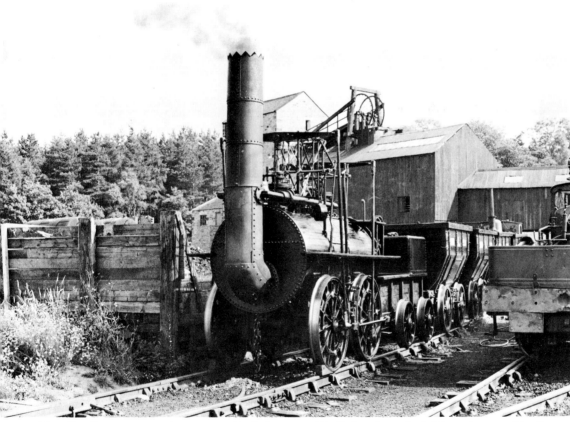

Left: An evocative glimpse of steam's early years, recreated at the North of England Open Air Museum, at Beamish. This working reproduction of George Stephenson's *Locomotion* of 1825, built in 1975, is pictured at the Beamish Colliery with a train of contemporary coal wagons, on August 26 1983. It was the opening of the Stockton & Darlington Railway for the carrying of coal which sparked widescale development of railways. *Nigel Harris.*

Not all railway companies were entirely happy with their role as freight carriers, and in the later years of the 19th century a rather patrician attitude to goods traffic was shown by the London & North Western Railway, which thought that its first class passengers must be shielded from the distasteful sight of the common goods train, and constructed screens at some of its main line stations to conceal their passing from customers standing on the platform! Nevertheless, even the LNWR had come to appreciate the financial importance of its goods business and whilst it still remained slightly aloof, the company was inextricably dependent on freight for survival.

To ensure development, the railways needed freight traffic revenue as much as the industries they served depended on reliable and rapid transport to stimulate their own growth. The good health of one partner was essential for the well-being of the other, and as the 19th century progressed this mutually-dependent expansion gained in both pace and momentum. For example, in the north, haematite (iron ore) was transported from West Cumberland through very

difficult country to Durham, via the Cockermouth Keswick & Penrith Railway, driven through the heart of the Lake District, and the South Durham & Lancashire Union Railway, which climbed 1,300ft over bleak Stainmore Summit. In return, coke from the coalfields of the north east was shipped to fuel the West Cumberland iron furnaces. In South Wales, vast quantities of coal for export were taken by train down the valleys to the coastal ports, where foreign iron ore, which the advent of steam shipping had made cheap to import, was then loaded and transported to the iron and steelworks of the region.

Before the Great Northern Railway came to London, coals from Newcastle had arrived by ship, and was unloadd at the West India Docks into the trains of the North London Railway, for delivery to the capital's suburbs. The GNR saw the commercial possibilities and, soon after its arrival in London, opened in 1851 a depot at King's Cross for the sale of Yorkshire coal. Better transport by steam power both on land and sea enabled coal to be moved to all corners of the kingdom, where it both fuelled industrial development and burned in the firegrates of its workforce, whose homes were also illuminated by gas produced from coal at the local gasworks. The development of industry and the expansion of railways was fuelled principally by the country's massive coal deposits, and for many years the railways carried more than 200 million tons annually, South Wales alone accounting for about 60 million tons.

In addition to their staple mineral traffic the railways also carried a significant amount of wagon-load freight, together with other smaller consignments, and receipts were substantial. However, seeds were being sown which ultimately resulted not only in major operational problems on a daily basis, but more seriously, much-restricted development of the goods train generally, and its motive power. Whilst passenger train weights and speeds developed and increased quickly, especially after the turn of the 20th century with more widespread use of bogie coaches and continuous brakes, the goods train plodded on as it always had done, admittedly heavier, but certainly no faster to any significant degree. By the 1930s, when Gresley's and Stanier's sophisticated and finely-engineered 'Pacifics' were running at record 'three-figure' speeds and express services were regularly running at speeds well into the '80s' and even '90s', the goods train (apart from a few specific exceptions like the LNER's 'Green Arrow' service of 1936) was still lumbering along at speeds of 15-30mph. Why had development become 'frozen' in this way?

Part of the problem was that overall distances travelled by goods trains were generally short, compared with countries like the United States of America, where long-haul goods traffic had prompted the development of huge bogie wagons and big locomotives. In this country, apart from special traffic for which specialised vehicles were provided, freight travelled in four-wheeled wagons constructed on a short wheelbase of around 10ft, and at their height, there were nearly one and a quarter million wagons of this type in service in this country, of which roughly half were privately owned by the mining companies and other regular customers. Unsprung or 'dumb' buffers were banned for main line use in 1913, but where axle bearings were lubricated by grease rather than oil, overheating occurred and affected wagons were shunted into sidings for subsequent repair and collection, causing extensive problems for the railway companies.

Problems were also compounded by the very nature of the business itself. Coal was the principal traffic for many railways, both for industry and also for domestic use, with delivery from station yards and goods depots to domestic coal shed by horse and cart. Most towns wanted their own goods yard and the railways certainly wanted the business, so goods depots were usually placed along a main line according to the practical delivery radius of a horse and cart. Consequently, goods trains had to stop at frequent intervals to shunt loaded wagons into sidings, and collect the 'empties.' To save space and eliminate points in small yards, sidings frequently featured wagon turntables, which were built to accommodate the short 10ft wheelbase wagon, and this in itself discouraged the introduction of bigger wagons.

There were also just too many wagons. A useful feature of large depots was under-line storage bins, filled by bottom-emptying hopper wagons, but at less important yards small open wagons were retained by the local coal merchant to store his stock and this practice created a need for more wagons, more marshalling, more storage space and more operational difficulty than would have been the case if wagons had been immediately unloaded and returned to traffic. Before the 'pooling' of wagons became commonplace during the First World War, the railways also suffered immense difficulties in sorting wagons and returning them to their various owners and staggering mileages were recorded by empty stock workings for which their was no real purpose.

However, the principal stumbling block towards the use of bigger wagons was caused by the mine owners, whose loading equipment was designed to handle the traditional small wagon, and there was great reluctance to spend money on new facilities. The coal business simply stagnated. This was a great pity, for in the second half of the 19th century average speeds of goods trains, despite the difficulties caused by the wagons used, were not regarded as being unduly slow. The GNR ran goods trains from King's Cross to Liverpool between 9pm at night and 7.30am the following morning, achieving speeds of slightly less than 30mph on the main line to Retford. The GWR also ran 200-ton trains at similar speeds from London to Exeter, and other companies were running similar services.

In the 20th century, there were attempts by some companies, notably the GNR and NER before the Grouping and the GWR and the LNER after 1923, to introduce larger capacity wagons — but with only limited success. Even in the years between the Grouping and Nationalisation the inherent problems caused by widespread use short, four-wheeled, unbraked wagons remained as a thorn in the side of the operators. Ponderous goods trains, if they could not be run at night, had to be frequently turned off the main lines into loops and sidings to allow the expresses to

Below: Known to enthusiasts as the 'Derby Four', the Fowler 4F 0-6-0 was the Midland Railway's standard goods engine — simple and cheap to construct and maintain, easy to operate and a reliable hauler of everyday freight traffic. Here we see No. 43924 storming away from the Bronte village of Haworth, on the Keighley & Worth Valley Railway, in January 1986. This was the first locomotive to be rescued for preservation from Dai Woodham's scrapyard, in South Wales, in 1968.
Jim Winkley.

Right: Lancashire & Yorkshire Railway 'Ironclad' 0-6-0 No. 52044 passes time between duties in front of the former goods warehouse, now used as a locomotive workshop, in Haworth yard, Worth Valley Railway. *Chris Milner.*

Below: On May 17 1980, NBR 0-6-0 No. 673 *Maude* gleams in the sunshine at Kilmarnock, during its long trip from its base at Falkirk to Rainhill, to join the celebrations to mark the 150th anniversary of the opening of the Liverpool & Manchester Railway, in 1830. *John S. Whiteley.*

pass: where the goods traffic was especially intense, the installation of expensive four-track main lines became necessary. On these sections, the goods trains could amble along on the slow lines, whilst the faster passenger services could pass by unhindered.

Consequently, the goods locomotive was not aggressively developed in the same way as its express passenger shed-mate, which is strange, considering that it was the goods traffic which earned the profits! By far the most common and widespread goods engine was the 0-6-0, of which thousands were built. The 0-6-0 was popular for it was simple to build, straightforward to operate, relatively cheap to maintain, and its entire weight sat squarely over the driving wheels, giving two distinct advantages in service. When a locomotive starts to move a heavy train, there is a tendency for weight to be transferred to the rear, with the result that 0-6-0s settle firmly on the track for maximum traction. The same principle applies to any engine without trailing wheels, and 2-6-0s and 4-6-0s are also very capable at moving a heavy train from a standing start. Other types, like 2-6-4Ts, 2-6-2s and especially 4-6-2s, experience a shift of weight from the driving wheels to the rear carrying wheels when starting a heavy train, hence their tendency to slip. Goods wagons were unbraked and the 0-6-0 also had the advantage of having 100% adhesion available for controlling a lengthy train of up to 100 loose-coupled wagons. Locomotive brakes did not become common on most railways until the 1880s, before which the tender handbrake was the only means of control. The 0-6-0 tender engine became firmly established

through the 1860s and from the following decade the type grew steadily in size and weight, simply to keep pace with increasing train weights.

One of the oldest surviving examples of the classic 0-6-0 tender design is GWR '2301' class 'Dean Goods' 0-6-0 No. 2516 (built in 1897) preserved as a static exhibit in the GWR Museum, Swindon. Introduced in 1883, this class eventually numbered 280 examples, all built between 1883 and 1899. Originally built to run on 'saturated' (non-superheated) steam, superheating equipment was later fitted and many members of the class served overseas in both France and Middle East during he First World War; more than 100 were later requisitioned for war service in the Second World War. They worked all over the GWR system, firstly on main line goods duties, but in later years were more commonly found on lighter secondary route services and branch line duties. The 'Dean Goods' class survived in service until 1957.

In the industrial north of England, the Lancashire & Yorkshire Railway had a very substantial goods traffic in coal and other commodities associated with the textile industry, and had extensive need for the simple and reliable goods power offered by the 0-6-0 tender engine. Two LYR classes of this type survive in the 1980s: class 2F 'Ironclad' 0-6-0 No. 957 (built in 1887) on the Keighley & Worth Valley Railway and class 3F No. 1300 (built 1896) at Steamtown, Carnforth. The Worth Valley Railway's No. 957 (later BR No. 52044) achieved fame as one of the locomotives used to pull 'the old gentleman's train' in the EMI feature length film version of 'The Railway Children'. No. 957 was built to Barton Wright's design of 1887, of which 280 examples were built in the following 11 years. This engine was built for the LYR by contractors Beyer Peacock, of Gorton, Manchester, and it worked until May 1959 when it was withdrawn from Wakefield engine shed, and preserved, the 0-6-0 arriving on the KWVR in March 1965. In 1887, the year No. 957 was built, Barton Wright was succeeded as CME of the LYR by J.F. Aspinall, who introduced his own class of 0-6-0, and he subsequently rebuilt the older Barton Wright tender engines as 0-6-0 saddle tank engines for shunting and other light duties. Interestingly, one of these modified engines also survives on the Worth Valley Railway enabling visitors to appreciate the 'before and after' appearance of this design.

Another surviving example of the 0-6-0 tender type, and an engine with a fascinating history, is North British Railway No. 673 *Maude* (built 1891) preserved today in main line running order by the Scottish Railway Preservation Society, at Falkirk. Designated as NBR class 'C' (later LNER Class J36) this design was introduced in 1888 as a broad contemporary to Aspinall's class '3F'. The class eventually consisted of 168 examples, of which 25 engines (including *Maude*) rendered wartime service in France. *Maude* was named following repatriation and other names with wartime connections given to this group of engines were: *Somme, Mons, Allenby, Haig, Joffre* and *French,* the names commemorating the names of First World War military commanders and

Above: The origins of the GWR Museum, Swindon, as a Wesleyan chapel are very clear in this view of the display prior to opening in 1962, showing principal locomotive exhibits: (right to left) 'Star' 4-6-0 No. 4003 *Lode Star,* 'City' 4-4-0 No. 3717 *City of Truro* and 'Dean Goods' 0-6-0 No. 2516. *City of Truro* was removed from this Museum and restored to working order in 1985, 150th anniversary year of the GWR. *National Railway Museum.*

their battles.

It is surprising that so many examples of such an elderly class survived into the 1960s, and Nos. 65288 and 65345 worked until June 1967, to become Scotland's very last pair of working BR steam locomotives. *Maude*, as BR No. 65243, was withdrawn in July 1966 and is preserved today by the SRPS at Falkirk, from where the locomotive works occasionally on main line railtours. In 1984, *Maude* was selected to work with Stanier 'Black 5' 4-6-0s Nos. 44767 *George Stephenson* and 5407 on a new programme of steam services operated regularly during the summer months over the picturesque 'West Highland extension' from Fort William to Mallaig. However, this steeply-graded route proved to be rather too much for this veteran engine, and whilst the Mallaig line steam specials ran again in subsequent years, *Maude* was not recalled to Fort William.

However, by far the best-known, and certainly the biggest class of 0-6-0 goods tender engines built for use in this country was the Midland Railway's Fowler '4F' class, of which a grand total of 772 examples were built. For such a large and important class, which represented the final development of a long line of MR 0-6-0 tender engines, the '4F' had a relatively inauspicious start following the construction at Derby in 1911 of class pioneer No. 3835. A second engine was built but no further examples were built until 1917, by which time, in the midst of the First World War, the MR was struggling to keep its coal trains on the move. Older, under-powered 0-6-0s were being unmercifully 'flogged' at the head of coal trains of epic length, onto which highly unsuitable class 2 passenger 4-4-0s were also attached at times of particularly intense difficulty.

Mainly because of route availability problems for large engines, extremely heavy goods trains on the Midland trundled slowly around the system behind over-taxed 0-6-0s which had to work perpetually in pairs, just to keep the trains on the move. This was indeed the MR's famous 'small engine policy' in action. By the time of the Grouping, in 1923, 197 'Derby Fours' were already in service, with a further 575 being added in later years by the company's successor, the LMS. They ran in all parts of the LMS system before and after Nationalisation, and whilst the class did excellent work in some locations, they needed skilled and specialised driving, firing and maintenance if they were to perform well, and where enginemen failed to master their peculiarities they were very unpopular.

Below: Steam in Sussex: SR 'Q' class 0-6-0 goods locomotive No. 541 approaches Freshfield on December 3 1983 with the 12.40 train from Sheffield Park to Horsted Keynes. Designed by Maunsell and introduced in 1938 after his retirement, the 'Q' class locomotives were wholly traditional in concept and construction. *Peter Zabek*.

The two final designs of British 0-6-0 tender engines came very late and both were on the Southern Railway; Maunsell's 'Q' class 0-6-0 of 1938 and Bulleid's highly distinctive 'Q1' of 1942. In the latter years of Maunsell's tenure as CME of the SR, there was a need for engines of light axle loading for branch line and secondary working, to replace older classes. Maunsell, in poor health, produced the 'Q' 0-6-0, which did not actually appear until 1938, by which time his successor, O. V. S. Bulleid, was in office as CME. The 'Qs', like the later 'B1' 4-6-0s on the LNER, were a design which utilised a high number of standard parts, patterns, tools and components already in use for existing classes. The finished product was an 0-6-0 of wholly traditional appearance, although steam heating equipment was fitted to the 'Q' class, so that they could assist with passenger traffic as well as working goods trains. At this time, the steam locomotive was at its peak of development and operation, with crack expresses and streamlined locomotives performing marvellous feats — yet little of the experience and advances made since the turn of the century were applied with any enthusiasm in producing this very ordinary design.

By 1942, Bulleid was in full control of his department and his close relationship with SR General Manager Eustace Missenden meant that he had a virtually free hand when he was called on to answer an urgent need for a reliable and robust goods locomotive with a wide route availability, and of greater power than the 20-strong Maunsell 'Q' class. There were always constraints of course, and the SR Civil Engineer prohibited a locomotive weighing more than 54 tons, or a tender in excess of 39½ tons. Bulleid first decided that a large boiler and firebox were required, so working to the limits of the SR loading gauge, started with the 'Lord Nelson' firebox, shortened slightly to suit the purpose. The boiler barrel was then also made as large as possible, to ensure that the locomotive would not go short of steam.

Bulleid used the distinctive BFB 'Boxpok' wheels on the 'Q1', in place of normal spoked

Above: Oliver Bulleid's 'Q1' class 0-6-0s were revolutionary in appearance and quite unlike the rather pedestrian 'Q' class which preceeded them on the SR (See page 94). Produced in wartime, Bulleid designed the 'Q1' class to minimise weight, hence the lack of running boards, and the 'Q1s' were stark, functional and powerful. Sole survivor BR No. 33001, a member of the National Collection, is seen here at Freshfield, on the Bluebell Railway, with a late afternoon train from Sheffield Park on October 24 1982. *Mick Roberts.*

Above: NER 0-8-0 No. 2238 (Class Q6) stands in the shed yard at Grosmont, North Yorkshire Moors Railway, on May 29 1982. Designed for haulage of very heavy mineral trains, the locomotive conveys an unmistakeable aura of power.
John S. Whiteley.

wheels, within the same wheelbase as that used on the 'Q' class. Having given the 'Q1' the biggest boiler and firebox possible, by using standard parts as far as was practical, Bulleid discarded as much extra weight as possible, to keep the finished locomotive within the limits placed upon him. Having employed a fair proportion of conventional components and techniques thus far, Bulleid then finished the locomotive with an ample helping of his own innovative style. Running boards were not provided on the new engines and lightweight boiler cladding was pre-formed in square, box-like sections supported on the frames instead of the normal 'crinoline' framework, and the smokebox followed a similar, highly unconventional shape. The finished product was so utterly startling and non-conventional in appearance that William Stanier is reported to have been aghast when he first encountered the 'Q1'! Whatever the reaction to his new engines, Bulleid had achieved his aim: the new 0-6-0 design weighed just 45 tons 18cwt, and it worked extremely well, too.

The 'Q1s' also came as a shock to the footplatemen, for they too had never encountered anything quite like them before. In service they were a success from the outset: the large boiler and firebox generated massive amounts of steam and the engines seemed to display at work a power capability beyond their size. They were fiery machines of character and spirit which could also record high speeds when the need and opportunity arose, and they were generally popular with their crews, especially the firemen who discovered that their own work was not excessive, despite the high steaming rate and power output. Known as 'Charlies' to trainspotters, the class of 40 'Q1' 0-6-0s lasted in service until January 1966. Class pioneer No. C1 was withdrawn in May 1964 and was subsequently preserved as part of the National Collection. It is based on the Bluebell Railway. Considering that the 'Q' class introduced in 1938 had been so thoroughly traditional in outlook and construction, the 'Q1' brought the traditional British 0-6-0 goods engine to a very unusual conclusion.

A logical development of the 0-6-0 type was to fit a larger boiler and an extra pair of driving wheels to create an 0-8-0 tender engine, and the London & North Western Railway had been the first British company to make widespread use of this type, after 1892/3. The LNWR built large numbers of 0-8-0s in various classes and at the Grouping of 1923 no fewer than 295 0-8-0s were handed over to the newly-formed LMS, which continued to build new examples of the LNWR pattern, albeit with more modern boilers. The ultimate development of the LNWR 0-8-0 was the

LMS-built class 'G2' series of 60 engines built in 1921, of which pioneer No. 9395 is preserved as part of the National Collection.

The North Eastern Railway also used 0-8-0s for heavy goods haulage, two examples surviving today as preserved engines: NER Class T2 (LNER Class Q6) 0-8-0 No. 2238 of 1918 and NER Class T3 (LNER Class Q7) No. 901 of 1919. Built as no-nonsense prime movers for very heavy goods trains, the 'T2' had two cylinders compared with the the 'T3's' three-cylinder drive. The 'T2', introduced in 1913 by Vincent Raven, was a superheated version of the existing 'T' and 'T1' 0-8-0s, and the class was soundly built to steam hard, for long periods of sustained high poweroutput, with very heavy loads on the tender drawbar. They withstood any amount of 'flogging' without running short of steam and they were well-liked by footplatemen and shed fitters alike. They would thunder away all day, everyday, with a heavy train coupled to the tender drawhook. The preserved engine was withdrawn from Sunderland shed in 1967 as BR No. 63395 and sold to a scrap dealer in Blyth, and it appeared that the one-time class of 120 engines was going to disappear for ever. However, the North Eastern locomotive Preservation roup launched an intense campaign to raise funds and the purchase price of £2,300 (a significant sum in 1967) was collected in just five months. The engine is based on the North Yorkshire Moors Railway, where it went into service in June 1970.

The 0-8-0 was a machine of great power for main line goods haulage — but only at relatively low speeds of around 20mph. Where a company wanted its goods traffic to run at higher speeds, the addition of a leading pair of smaller carrying wheels was sensible, and the resulting 2-8-0 also became a popular British freight tender engine, especially on the LNER, GWR and LMS systems. The GWR also utilised eight-coupled main line tank engines for freight haulage, and examples of both the 2-8-0T and 2-8-2T types constructed at Swindon can still be seen today.

The 2-8-0 tender engine was introduced to this country by the GWR in 1903, with Churchward's '28xx' class, a two-cylinder locomotive. Major construction of the class started in 1905 and as first built, they were given full passenger livery of green, lined in black and orange, together with customary GWR complement of polished copper and brass, which included a gleaming cast numberplate on the cab sides. The tender sides carried the ornate 'belt and buckle' GWR coat-of-arms, flanked by the legend 'Great Western', and these engines must must have appeared majestic indeed, bedecked in such finery, at the head of a lengthy train of perhaps grubby privately owned coal wagons! The outbreak of war in 1914 brought an enforced end to such unnecessary adornment of goods engines, and the characteristic ornateness of the pre-First World War days was never reapplied to the GWR's goods fleet.

For the very heavy South Wales coal traffic, where tank engines were more appropriate than tender engines in view of the reverse-direction running required down the valleys, the GWR

Above: Churchward 2-8-0 No. 3822 on display on September 28 1985 at the Didcot Railway Centre, Oxfordshire, home of the Great Western Society. This class was introduced in 1903, although No. 3822 was not built until 1940. Mick Roberts.

Above: Heavyweight steam power on the Great Central Railway: GWR 2-8-0T No. 5224 takes water at Loughborough, April 6 1985.
John Cooper-Smith.

provided a 2-8-0T, starting with the '42xx' series of 1910. The '52xx' development of the class, introduced in 1923, had bigger cylinders and other detail differences to the original '42xx' engines but worked in the same capacity, principally in South Wales. They were the only 2-8-0Ts ever to work in Britain No. 5239 (built 1924), now named *Goliath*, is used regularly on the passenger trains of the the Torbay Steam Railway, running between Paignton and Kingswear, whilst sister 2-8-0T No. 5224 has also been restored to running order on the Great Central Railway (See also Chapter 9).

A series of 40 2-8-0Ts of the '52xx' series, built between December 1925 and October 1930, Nos. 5255-5294 were rebuilt from 1934 as class '72xx' 2-8-2T locomotives, and No. 7200, the first of the conversions, is today preserved at the Buckinghamshire Railway Centre, near Aylesbury. No. 7200 had been built in 1930 as 2-8-0T No. 5275 for the valleys coal traffic, but at this time

the world recession was causing declining production, and many 2-8-0Ts were without work. Transfer to other locations was impractical because of their limited coal and water capacity, so 40 examples were rebuilt as 2-8-2Ts, the biggest tank engines ever to work in this country. Thus modified they worked in many parts of the GWR system.

An early 20th century 2-8-0 of particular appeal was that produced by the Midland Railway, initially in 1914, for use on the Somerset & Dorset Joint Railway, and two later examples of this type, built in 1925, are still with us today. The 'S&D' was a sinuous, undulating cross-country route with many lengthy inclines, some as fierce as 1 in 50, and before the First World War there was heavy coal traffic between Bath and Radstock, and, in the summer months, many holiday excursions, bound for Bournemouth. After the war started in August 1914 the holiday 'extras' disappeared, but the heavy coal traffic intensified, whilst general freight, which included train loads of sheeted armaments and tanks, increased in the southbound direction. Double-heading had become a regular practice and a powerful freight locomotive was needed which could tackle

the increased loadings without having to recourse to expensive and wasteful second-engine working. The MR had been supplying motive power for the 'S&D' since 1875, so it was not surprising that Derby was asked to meet this requirement, but the resulting class 7F 2-8-0s were a little unusual in that the MR was happy to use nothing larger than an 0-6-0 for its own heavy freight traffic. However, the elegant 2-8-0s its draughtsmen produced were handsome, capable engines which became a hall-mark of 'S&D' operations for the next 50 years.

Ever economical in outlook, the MR used standard parts and patterns wherever possible and the '7Fs' boiler was identical to that used on the standard 'Compound' 4-4-0. Six engines were built, originally Nos. 80-85, and they were unusual, by Derby's normal standards, in being the first two-cylinder design built by the MR where the cylinders were mounted on the outside of the main frames, and the first Derby engines with outside Walschaerts valve gear. A further five examples, with slightly larger boilers, were constructed in 1925 by Stephenson & Co. Ltd., but these engines subsequently received smaller boilers of the type fitted to the original class of six.

The 'S&D' 2-8-0s were sure-footed and very powerful, and they had a very distinctive Derby 'look' about them — they were every inch the 'big brother' of the '4F' with which the parent Company persisted to entrust its own goods traffic. In the 1950s, the 2-8-0s were frequently pressed into passenger service over the 'S&D' where they were capable of single-handedly hauling 10 coaches, compared with the six-coach limit applied to the LMS class 5 4-6-0s and even Bulleid's 'Pacifics'. They were indeed a credit to their designers and it is impossible to talk of the lamented 'S&D', which closed in March 1966, without thinking of the 2-8-0s as the route's unforgettable 'trade-mark.'

In the leisure market of the 1980s, the once-humble goods engine which in service rarely warranted a second glance has become the 'Cinderella' of the steam business. It is now polished and groomed alongside the more glamorous passenger classes, with which it takes its equal turn at the head of trains of carriages, on private railways all over the country. In Yorkshire, on the five-mile Keighley & Worth Valley Railway, and in the Midlands, on the Severn Valley Railway, can be seen working examples of a freight class which also served its country well— the Stanier Class 8F 2-8-0. Introduced in 1935, the '8F' was Stanier's answer to the LMS requirement for a modern, powerful goods engine, to tackle the most arduous workings then in the hands of LNWR 0-8-0 and MR 0-6-0 classes, together with a variety of goods and mixed traffic engines inherited from the other pre-Grouping constituents. The first '8F' (actually classified '7F' when first introduced) emerged from Crewe works in summer 1935, carrying the number 8000.

Following the outbreak of war in September 1939, the Stanier 2-8-0 was selected as a Ministry of Supply standard goods locomotive and 230 new examples were ordered from a variety of contractors. The modified MoS '8Fs' were sent instead to the Middle East, where they did much useful work. Oil-burning equipment was fitted to 90 examples, which were despatched to Iran, others were used in Egypt and Palestine.

Later in the war, when increasing numbers of heavy goods engines were needed to meet traffic requirements at home, the non-LMS railway works at Swindon, Ashford, Eastleigh, Doncaster, Brighton and Darlington were ordered to assist Crewe and Horwich in building new '8F' 2-8-0s. After 1943, the standard goods engine role for overseas and home duty was taken over by the Robert Riddles 'Austerity' design, described in Chapter 8.

A total of 849 Stanier '8F' 2-8-0s were built, some of the overseas engines returning to work in the country after 1945, and following Nationalisation their BR number series was 48000-48775. The unsung workhorses of the London Midland goods scene (though at busy periods they deputised on passenger trains, occasionally at speeds of up to 60mph) the '8F' 2-8-0s specialised in long-haul mineral workings. The first withdrawal occurred in 1960, and despite steady erosion in subsequent years, a handful remained at work to the very end, based at Carnforth, Lostock Hall (Preston) and especially Rose Grove, where they were renowned for their 'last stand' workings with coal trains over the steeply-graded Copy Pit route, between Burnley and Todmorden. A survivor at the very end at Rose Grove shed was No. 48773, which was preserved after withdrawal in 1968 and now runs on the Severn Valley Railway as LMS No. 8233. Built for War Department service in 1940, this locomotive worked for the LMS until 1941, when as No. 307 it went to Iran and subsequently Egypt, the engine returning to this country as WD No. 500 in 1952. The 2-8-0 worked on the Longmoor Military Railway for five years, before transfer to BR service as No. 48773 in 1957. Other surviving '8F' class locomotives are listed in Chapter 9.

Above: American-built 'S160' 2-8-0 No. 5820 approaches Oakworth, Keighley & Worth Valley Railway on September 6 1981, with a passenger train en-route from Keighley to Oxenhope. Known on the KWVR as 'Big Jim' No. 5820 is one of several hundred examples shipped to Europe for service during the Second World War. Locomotives of this class worked in this country, although No. 5820, built in Lima, Ohio in 1945, worked in Poland, from where it was bought and transported to Keighley in November 1977. This locomotive starred in the feature film 'Yanks' filmed on location around Keighley in 1978.
Tim Grimshaw.

CHAPTER 7:
TANK ENGINES

Above: LNWR 'Coal' tank No. 1054 leads its three coach train towards Oxenhope, after leaving Haworth, Worth Valley Railway, on July 26 1986. This popular 0-6-2T, built in 1888, is normally based at the Dinting Railway Centre. *Peter Millar.*

To many people, it is the fussing little tank engine which epitomises the friendly appeal of the steam locomotive, and many thousands of small tank engines of four and six-wheel outline spent frequently lengthy lives shunting wagons and coaches in sidings and goods yards. However, many quite large examples were also designed for a variety of main line duties, from humble freight trains to short-distance fast, passenger workings.

The great advantage of the tank engine was its flexibility of operation. By carrying its coal and water in bunkers and tanks mounted on the same frame as the boiler, a generally shorter locomotive could be built than a tender engine of similar capacity. The tender engine also worked best when running smokebox-first, and turning a locomotive to face the required direction of travel was not always possible or convenient. The tank engine did not necessarily need to run smokebox-first and was equally at home running in reverse with either goods or passenger trains, and were thus especially well-suited to branch line duties.

Whilst the first British tank engines appeared during the 1830s, they were not built in large numbers until the 1850s and after, and even then were used mainly for shunting, branch line operation and short distance trips over main lines. During the 1860s however, the sprawling suburbs of London started to generate a passenger traffic which was destined to grow into the hugely complex commuter operations of today. These services were characterised by brisk running between closely-spaced stations, and their locomotives needed to be capable of sharp acceleration away from frequent stops.

The increasing demands of the LSWR suburban passenger service after 1880 prompted the introduction of a class 71 4-4-2Ts, designed by W. Adams and built between 1882 and 1885. Of classic Victorian lines and extremely elegant in appearance, the class was extinct on the SR by 1928 with the exception of two examples retained to work the Axminster-Lyme Regis branch, for whose tortuous curves the Adams 4-4-2Ts were particularly suitable. Under normal circumstances, the class would have vanished by 1930, and it is entirely due to the highly specific requirements of the Lyme Regis branch that the Adams 4-4-2Ts survived. The sole preserved member of this class, withdrawn from Exmouth Junction shed in July 1961 as BR No. 30583, has a history of particular interest.

Built in 1885, this locomotive was sold by the LSWR as being surplus to requirements in September 1917, when the Ministry of Munitions acquired it for £2,104. In 1919 the 4-4-2T was re-sold for just £900 to the East Kent Railway, where it remained at work until 1939, when it was placed in store. In 1946 the Southern Railway bought the engine for £800 and following a complete overhaul, the 4-4-2T re-entered service on the Lyme Regis branch alongside its two surviving sister engines. The trio remained together, shuttling back and forth through the idyllic Dorset countryside, until they were finally replaced at the end of 1961 by Ivatt Class 2MT 2-6-2Ts. Nos. 30582 and 30584 were both dismantled for scrap at Eastleigh Works, whilst No.

Below: Climbing Fresh-field Bank, on the Bluebell Railway, on March 5 1983 is LSWR 4-4-2T No. 30583, painted in the BR lined black livery in which it ended its working days on the Lyme Regis branch in July 1961. *Mike Pope.*

30583 was rescued for preservation on the Bluebell Railway, where it can still be seen today, now in its second century of existence.

The 0-6-0T was always a popular tank engine design, though more usually utilised for shunting and freight work, rather than passenger service. This applied particularly in the later parts of the 19th century and after, but in the 1870s, when suburban train weights were still relatively light, an 0-6-0T capable of sharp acceleration was a useful asset. In October 1872, Locomotive Superindent William Stroudley introduced his famous 'Terrier' class A1 0-6-0T, later rebuilt as class A1X. Between 1872 and 1880 the LBSCR built 50 engines of this class, which were very small in outline, with a tall chimney and short side tanks of just 500 gallons capacity. They were snappy performers on the suburban traffic of the day, but were superseded as train weights increased, and some examples had been scrapped soon after the turn of the century.

Were it not for their diminutive size and deceptive power, the class would have vanished more than 80 years ago, but a handful were retained for specialised service, or were sold for private industrial use, enabling them to survive long enough for preservationists to secure their future. The only engine to survive in this country in original condition, with a short smokebox, is the National Railway Museum's No. 82 *Boxhill*, built in 1880 and retained by the SR after Nationalisation for use as Brighton Works shunter. It was withdrawn in 1946 and preserved. Of the 'A1X' rebuilds, two examples can be found on the Bluebell Railway, each with a very different background providing the reason for survival. The oldest engine is LBSCR No. 72 *Fenchurch*, built at Brighton in 1872 at a cost of £500 as the very first of Stroudley's 'Terriers'. In

Below: An evocative scene on the Kent & East Sussex Railway as Terrier' No. 32670 approaches Rolvenden with a demonstration goods train on the Spring Bank Holiday Sunday of 1985. This is a beautifully recreated scene of the country railway of the steam era.
Peter Zabek.

1898 it was sold to the Newhaven Harbour Company, which in 1925 was taken over by the Southern Railway, the 'Terrier' being taken into stock as No. B636. Renumbered 32636 by BR after 1948, the locomotive was finally withdrawn from Eastleigh shed in November 1963, when it was bought by the Bluebell Railway. Sister engine LBSCR No. 55 *Stepney* was built in 1875, and remained in service with the LBSCR and SR. becoming BR No. 32655 in 1948 and working until withdrawal from Eastleigh in May 1960, after which it was preserved on the Bluebell Railway. This locomotive is painted in Stroudley yellow livery and has been immortalised in the 'Railway Series' of books by the Reverend Wilbert Awdry. Other preserved 'Terriers' are detailed in Chapter 9.

The 0-6-2 side tank was popular and a unique survivor today is London & North Western Railway 0-6-2T No. 1054, built in 1881 to a design introduced in 1881 by F. W. Webb. Known as 'Coal tanks' these locomotives, designed primarily for goods traffic, were nevertheless frequently used as passenger engines and were of true mixed traffic capability. Extremely versatile in service, 300 examples were built between 1881 and 1896, of which only 52 did not survive long enough to receive LMS numbers after the Grouping of 1923. All were scrapped by the mid 1950s, apart from BR No. 58926, which lasted until 1958. Based latterly at Shrewsbury by BR, on January 5 1958 No. 58926 was chartered to haul a 'last train' special working over the Abergavenny-Merthyr line, after which most sections of this route were closed. Now owned by the National Trust and restored in LNWR livery as No. 1054, the 'Coal tank' is maintained in main line running order by the Dinting Railway Centre. Examples of other 0-6-2T classes from the North Staffordshire and Taff Vale Railways also survive, as shown in Chapter 9.

In 1889, the LSWR introduced larger 0-4-4Ts designed by W. Adams and built at Nine Elms for branch line working and short distance passenger work. Known later as class '02', a number of these engines were transferred to the Isle of Wight to work air-braked passenger services, and because of this specialised use a handful of engines lasted long enough for a single example,

Above: Sole survivor of the LSWR class '02' 0-4-4Ts is No. 24 Calbourne, seen here painted in SR green livery, shunting the yard at Haven Street, on the Isle of Wight Steam Railway in September 1981. IOWSR steam trains run over a 1¾-mile length of track from the beautifully restored Victorian station at Haven Street, which in 1987 won the premier award in the annual Association of Railway Preservation Societies competition for the best restored station. Mike Pope.

Right: The Lancashire & Yorkshire Railway built 330 of these 2-4-2Ts, which competently handled passenger traffic of all types, from local 'stopping' trains to fast expresses. This view shows No. 31, in LYR days, at work in the Calder Valley. Class pioneer No. 1008 survives at the National Railway Museum, York.
Silver Link Collection.

Right: The Lancashire & Yorkshire Railway built 330 of these 2-4-2Ts, which competently handled passenger traffic of all types, from local 'stopping' trains to fast expresses. This view shows No. 31, in LYR days, at work in the Calder Valley. Class pioneer No. 1008 survives at the National Railway Museum, York.
Silver Link Collection.

Below: The 0-4-4T remained popular for suburban passenger duties, as illustrated by Metropolitan Railway No. 1, preserved today at the Buckinghamshire Railway Centre. *Mick Roberts.*

LSWR No. W24 *Calbourne* (built 1891) to be preserved. Originally a class of 60 engines, only 48 remained at work at the time of Nationalisation, which included 21 examples on the Isle of Wight, numbered in the series, W14-W34 and named after places of local interest. By 1957, the class had been whittled down to 37 examples, of which 18 were working in the mainland, and 19 were on the Isle of Wight, where the '02s' attracted much attention after 1960, when their IoW services, featuring ancient and antiquated passenger stock were of great appeal to the railway photographer. During the 1960s, the class was concentrated at Ryde shed until their last year of service in 1967, when the last pair were Nos. W24 *Calbourne* and W31 *Chale*: both had been withdrawn by March. *Chale* was scrapped but *Calbourne* was preserved by the Wight Locomotive Society and after a few years in store at Newport, the 0-4-4T was moved to Haven Street Station, where the WLS established the Isle of Wight Steam Railway.

Although 0-4-4Ts were capable of relatively high speed, it became generally accepted that leading carrying wheels gave smoother riding and better stability, and just as 0-6-0s and 0-8-0s became 2-6-0s and 2-8-0s, the tank engines also grew apace. However, as a result of the requirement to run equally well in either direction, carrying wheels were added both in front and behind the main driving wheels to produce a range of different, new types. In the north of

England, the Lancashire & Yorkshire Railway operated a wide range of relatively short, but fast passenger services, with plenty of station calls, with a very successful 2-4-2 design, of which a single example survives as a non-working exhibit in the National Collection.

Introduced in 1889 by J. A. F. Aspinall, the preserved 2-4-2T No. 1008 was not only the first of its 2-4-2 class, it was also the first engine to be built at the then-new LYR workshops at Horwich, near Bolton. The Aspinall 2-4-2 was extremely successful in service and by 1898 there were 210 examples in service. The design was subsequently improved by the addition of superheaters, bigger bunkers and larger water tanks. Eventually the LYR built 330 of these very useful locomotives, which worked all over its trans-Pennine system on a very wide range of duties, including front line services normally handled by larger locomotives of 4-6-0 and 4-4-2 wheel arrangements. Withdrawal of this class started under LMS ownership in 1928, but the class survived into BR ownership (No. series 50621-50899) and the last examples were not scrapped until 1961. The NRM example was officially preserved in view of its historic status, following withdrawal from Manningham shed, Yorkshire, in October 1954.

In the early part of the 20th century, a wider appreciation of the principle and application of steam superheating enabled passenger tank engines to develop fully into fast and versatile classes of useful endurance, for the superheating of steam to very high temperatures extracted much more work from each gallon of water, which consequently lasted much longer. Already in limited supply on any tank engine design, any technical improvement which made water last longer was a significant advantage. Whereas the first part of this chapter provided a brief survey of chiefly late 19th century tank engine designs by looking at different wheel arrangements, it is more convenient to look at the remaining 20th century passenger designs through a company-by-company survey of the 'Big Four' of the pre 1948 era, and their constituents. This is especially useful in the case of the GWR, which in the years following Churchward's appointment as CME in 1902, pursued a strong policy of standardisation.

The most common GWR suburban tank engine type was the 2-6-2 ('Prairie') of varying classes and capacities. Today, three different classes of 'Prairie' tank survive, of the '45xx', '51xx' and '61xx' series, including some examples in working order. The '45xx' so-called 'Small Prairie' was introduced in 1906 and eight members of this class survive today. Churchward designed the '45xx' engines for light passenger work, especially on the sharply curved branch lines of the west country, and in due course they were seen in most parts of the GWR system. They were especially common in Devon and Cornwall. The class became extinct in general service during 1964, but many examples were despatched to Barry for scrap, where they lingered in Woodham's dock sidings long enough for preservationists to start rescuing them.

Subsequent GWR 2-6-2T designs were of larger weight, power and capacity, and examples of

Above: A popular performer on the Severn Valley Railway is GWR 'small Prairie' No. 4566, seen here leaving Foley Park tunnel with the 11.30am departure from Kidderminster, on December 20 1986. This locomotive, built in 1924, was bought from Barry scrapyard in 1970 for use on the SVR and restored to working order at the Railway's workshops at Bridgnorth. *Peter Zabek.*

Above: In 1986, the Didcot Railway Centre's classic GWR branch line locomotive, Collett Class '14xx' 0-4-2T No. 1466 was loaned to the Llangollen Railway, in Clwyd. The diminutive locomotive is seen here leaving Llangollen with a three-coach train on July 29 1986. *Andrew Bell.*

the '51xx' and '61xx' series can still be seen today to enable comparisons to be drawn. On the Severn Valley Railway for example, 'Small Prairie' No. 4566 (a small water capacity engine of 57 tons weight) can be compared with '51xx' class engines Nos. 4141 and 5164, which weigh more than 78 tons. The '51xx' 'Prairies' were allocated to suburban duties all over the GWR territory before and after Nationalisation, but in the late 1950s they started to be displaced by new diesel multiple units, and withdrawals commenced. By 1965, the GWR's 'Prairie' tanks were extinct. Surviving 'Prairies' of both '51xx' and '61xx' groups are listed in Chapter 9.

The GWR was noted for its high number of country branch lines, and the classic branch line locomotive was the Collett '14xx' class 0-4-2T, introduced in August 1932. These small, highly attractive engines epitomised the English country branch line, as depicted so affectionately in the famous Ealing comedy 'The Titfield Thunderbolt,' which featured one of the Collett 0-4-2Ts. Initially numbered in the '48xx' series, this class of 75 examples was fitted with 'push-pull' equipment to eliminate frequent 'running round' operations over short branch and other rural routes, where frequent reversals were necessary. The image of one of these engines, later renumbered in the '14xx' series, coupled to a single auto-trailer became the enduring hall-mark of GWR branch line tradition, and has been recreated in modern times both on the Dart Valley Railway, and at the Didcot Railway Centre, where preserved examples can be found. Withdrawals started in 1956 and continued for the next nine years, and in 1965 Western Region withdrew from Exmouth Junction its last pair of '14xx' 0-4-2Ts, Nos. 1450 and 1442. No. 1442 was purchased for static preservation at Tiverton Museum, Devon, where it remains today, whilst No. 1450 went to the Dart Valley Railway, where it was named *Ashburton*. Sister 0-4-2T No. 1420, now named *Bulliver*, can also be found on the DVR, at Buckfastleigh. The last member of the preserved '14xx' quartet is No. 1466, maintained in working order by the Great Western Society, at Didcot.

A good example of the LNER 0-6-2T suburban locomotive is the Gresley 'N2' 0-6-2T LNER No. 4744, built in 1921 and maintained today as a working locomotive on the Great Central Railway. The 'N2' was a Gresley development of the 'N1' 0-6-2T designed by Ivatt and introduced in 1907, for suburban services from King's Cross. In all, 107 'N2' 0-6-2Ts were built, some of which were

Left: LMS-design Fairburn 2-6-4T No. 2085 stands in front of the Furness Railway station buildings and goods shed at Haverthwaite, on Cumbria's Lakeside & Haverthwaite Railway, in May 1983, during the Railway's tenth anniversary celebrations. No. 2085 is carrying the lined blue livery of the Caledonian Railway. Sister Fairburn 2-6-4T No. 2073 is also based on the LHR. *Alan Middleton.*

Below: On June 16 1985, class '57XX' GWR 0-6-0PT No. 9681 nears Norchard, Dean Forest Railway, with a tree-clearance works train from Lydney. Designed by GWR CME C.B. Collett, this locomotive was actually built in 1949, after Nationalisation. *Mick Roberts.*

fitted with exhaust condensing apparatus for working in the Metropolitan tunnels. No. 4744, originally GNR No. 1744 and numbered 69523 after 1948, was withdrawn from Peterborough in 1962 and transferred intially to the Keighley & Worth Valley Railway. Subsequently moved to the GCR, No. 4744 is owned by the Gresley Society.

The LMS made extensive use of large suburban tank engines, and under Fowler and Stanier utilised high boiler pressure and a high degree of steam superheating to create a suburban tank engine capable of very high speed, based on the 2-6-4T wheel arrangement. Charles Fairburn took over from Stanier as CME of the LMS in 1944, and had barely a year in office before he died and was succeeded by H. G. Ivatt, who occupied the position until the LMS ceased to exist at the end of 1947. Fairburn's only 'new' design was his development of the tried and trusted Stanier two-cylinder 2-6-4T, first introduced in 1935, and of which more than 200 examples were built. Fairburn's modified design followed the basic proportions of the Stanier class, and was similar in appearance in many ways, the chief technical difference being a shorter coupled wheelbase, enablingthe new 2-6-4Ts to negotiate a curve of five chains radius, compared with the six chains radius limit of the Stanier engines. The class was multiplied by both LMS and BR, and by 1951 277 examples were in traffic, and amongst the last batch, built in the former LBSCR Works at Brighton, were Nos. 42073 and 42085, the pair preserved on the LHR.

Thus far we have examined the tank engines designed and constructed for passenger operations of secondary, suburban and branch line workings; we shall now turn to the wide variety of other, generally small-wheeled types, used either for shunting or short-distance haulage of goods trains. Whereas not all companies of the pre-Grouping era needed express passenger classes, such as the coal-carrying railways of South Wales, they all, without exception, needed small tank classes and a variety of these locomotives are still with us today. The GWR made extensive use of the pannier tank type, which was still being developed at Swindon on the very eve of Nationalisation, the last new design not appearing until 1949, under BR auspices

Not all pannier tank designs introduced by the GWR are represented today, but classes introduced chiefly for shunting can be found at the Buckinghamshire Railway Centre and the Dart Valley Railway. At the Buckinghamshire Railway Centre can be found immaculately restored '94xx' 0-6-0PT No. 9466, designed by Hawksworth for heavy shunting and introduced in February 1947. The '94xx' pannier tank engines weighed more than 55 tons and were used on all parts of the former GWR system: class leader No. 9400 is a static exhibit in the GWR Museum,Swindon and No. 9466 is the only other preserved example. Withdrawn in July 1964, No. 9466 lay at Barry docks until June 1975, when it was privately purchased and moved to the BRC site at Quainton, near Aylesbury. Using a rudimentary workshop established in a box van, owner Dennis Howells restored to 9466 to pristine condition in the open air, disproving any belief that a shed and sophisticated facilities are essential to complete a quality restoration.

The '16xx' class had been designed as a lighter alternative to the standard '57xx' class 0-6-0PT design, of which in the late 1950s no fewer than 860 examples were in service for BR — numerically the largest single class of locomotives. The '57xx' class was designed as a standard engine, capable of bulk production to replace a wide range of older and more diverse classes of similar capacity. There was a hardly a station, goods yard, branch line or main line in GWR territory on which they were not common, either before or after Nationalisation. They were shunters of powerful capabilities, but they also worked branch traffic, local passenger turns and assisted with double heading and 'banking' duties on steeply graded routes. The '57xx' 0-6-0PTs were also used on the Southern Region after Nationalisation, and in passenger service they were capable of speeds of up to 65 mph. The encroaching tide of dieselisation from the late 1950s gradually displaced the ubiquitous '57xx' class,and the familiar pattern of withdrawal and scrapping proceeded. They dwindled rapidly after 1962: 172 were scrapped during that year, 112 more were condemned in 1963, 144 in 1964 and 140 in 1965. A handful of 27 survivors steamed into 1966, but by November they had all gone. Today, 16 examples of this once-extensive class survive, although the much-cannibalised No. 9629 only as a cosmetically restored 'hulk' in the grounds of the Holiday Inn, Cardiff. The other survivors are detailed in Chapter 9.

The '57xx' 0-6-0PTs fulfilled a role traditionally occupied by the six-wheeled tank engine since the second half of the 19th century, and amongst the surviving steam locomotives of the LMS group of companies can be found one of its oldest working examples — North London Railway 0-6-0T No. 2650. Preserved by the Bluebell Railway, this outside-cylinder side tank locomotive was built in 1880 to a design introduced in 1879 by J. C. Park, for light suburban freight and shunting duties. Five members of the class survived into the late 1950s, some having been moved north to work the legendary Cromford & High Peak Railway, which featured the sharpest curves and steepest sections of adhesion- worked standard gauge railway anywhere in the United Kingdom, the notorious Hopton Incline featuring a 200-yard section graded at 1 in 14! Four of the NLR tanks had been withdrawn by 1958, leaving No. 58850 in service, this engine remaining at Rowsley, where engines for the CHPR had been based, until September 1960 when it too was withdrawn. Happily, the locomotive was preserved and can still be seen at work on the Bluebell Railway. Shunting engine designs were generally modernised as the years passed, as witnessed by the development of the GWR's pannier tank types, and the growth of small MR 0-6-0Ts into the 'Jinty' class of the LMS. However, in other cases designs remained unchanged for extremely long periods and a particularly startling example is the 0-6-0T designed by Wilson Worsdell for the NER in 1898, later classified as 'J72' by the LNER, and which was still being built by British

Above: A volcanic display on the Bluebell Railway's Freshfield Bank, on February 1 1987, as LSWR class B4 0-4-0T *Normandy* forges upgrade with the 2.30 pm Horsted Keynes — Sheffield Park train. The column of steam at the rear indicates the presence of a 'banker' — in this instance, North London Railway 0-6-0T No. 58850. *Mike Esau.*

Left: Class J72 0-6-0T No. 69023 *Joem* and 0-6-0ST No. 62 tackle the 1 in 49 gradient from Grosmont to Goathland, on the North Yorkshire Moors Railway, with a Pickering-bound train of May 29 1984. *Gavin Morrison.*

Railways after Nationalisation in 1951! The last batch of locomotives were built to precisely the same design as the first examples, constructed 53 years earlier to meet the shunting requirements of the late 19th century! A solitary preserved example is BR No. 69023 *Joem* owned by the North Eastern Locomotive Preservation Group and based on the North Yorkshire Moors Railway.

Although constructed over a 53-year span, the 'J72' class was not numerically large, compared with other classes built over much shorter periods, and a total of 113 examples were built at railway workshops at Darlington and Doncaster, and the Armstrong Whitworth works at Newcastle. In 1898, the 'J72' class cost just £1,412 per engine and by 1951 this figure had risen to £5,314. NELPG's No. 69023, one of the last batch built at Darlington in 1951, was withdrawn from service in October 1964, when the class became officially extinct. However, Nos.69023 and 69005 were retained for departmental use by BR, ensuring their survival until final withdrawal in 1967, when Leeds businessman Ronald Ainsworth purchased No. 69023. It is now owned by the North Eastern Locomotive Preservation Group.

The first steam locomotives of the early 19th century were built for industrial use, and the 'works shunters' which were once such a familiar sight around Britain have a longer history and pedigree than any other type of railway locomotive. Cornishman Richard Trevithick is generally credited with having built the first industrial steam locomotive in 1804 for the Pen-y-Darren mine, Stephenson is usually accepted as being the father of the railway in general and the steam locomotive in particular. Despite Trevithick's early work with industrial steam, it was only after the 1850s that industrial development and the expansion of railways generally reacted together to produce the ideal environment for the development of the privately-owned works locomotive.

The railway enabled industries to bring in their raw materials efficiently and easily, and provided a method for the despatch of the finished product, and it was logical that sidings should be laid around the factories or mines to facilitate production. Industrial users were encouraged to own their own wagons (which, incidentally, paved the way for the problems which later afflicted the railway's goods business, described in Chapter 6) and also their own locomotives, which at first had running rights over main lines. Eventually however, it became standard practice to lay a set of 'exchange sidings' into which the main line companies delivered empty wagons and collected loaded trains, leaving the works shunter to carry out internal marshalling.

The 'boom period' for industrial steam locomotive builders occurred in the latter half of the

19th century, when nearly every industrial conurbation included a locomotive factory. At their peak, more than 70 different private companies built small tank engines, principally of four and six-wheeled construction, for use in private sidings and yards.

Each manufacturer had its own standard locomotives and distinctive styles and their products were built to be robust and reliable in difficult circumstances. Industrial locations frequently featured very sharp curves or lightly-laid track and some engines were of very short wheelbase and comparatively lightweight construction, whilst others were heavier machines designed for short-distance 'slogging' with heavy trains in steelworks or collieries, for example. Industrial track became legendary for its poor quality and alignment, with curves consisting of a series of straight lines and sharp angles, laid usually without ballast, and resulting in 'dips and bumps' of spectacular appearance.

Industrial locomotives for British use were generally of 0-4-0 and 0-6-0 wheel arrangements, and featured side, saddle, well and pannier tanks. They could be long or short in length, tall or squat in height, and extremely variable in weight, cylinder size, power output and appearance. Painted in all shades of the rainbow and named after an amazing variety of subjects from battleships and Greek Gods to the directors' daughters of their erstwhile owners, preserved industrial shunting locomotives illustrate an important aspect of British railway history, which at its zenith was largely unappreciated, even by many railway enthusiasts.

CHAPTER 8:
BR 'STANDARD' LOCOMOTIVES

It is impossible to discuss the range of 'Standard' steam locomotives — a total of 999 locomotives in 12 different classes — built for British Railways after Nationalisation in 1948, without discussing the career of their designer, Robert Riddles, the former LMS locomotive engineer who had worked as an assistant to the great William A. Stanier. However, whilst Riddles is best remembered for his 'Standard' locomotives, he had two main line classes to his credit before Nationalisation — the renowned Ministry of Supply 'Austerity' 2-8-0s and 2-10-0s built during the Second World War, and known to a generation of enthusiasts simply as 'WDs', as a result of their War Department parentage.

These locomotives, built at minimum cost, ostensibly for short term service during the war, actually served for more than 20 years after the end of hostilities in 1945, some examples surviving until the very end of steam traction on BR metals in 1968. That locomotives of both types can be seen in steam and at work in this country in the 1980s is a tribute to the preservation movement, for two of the four MoS locomotives currently preserved within these shores were actually bought from the Greek railways and shipped back to this country in non-working order, whilst a third was imported from Sweden! The only 'Austerity' 2-8-0 in Britain is based on the Keighley & Worth Valley Railway, whilst in early 1987 the 2-10-0s could be found at the Severn Valley Railway, in the West Midlands, and on Hampshire's Mid Hants Railway.

During the second World War, Riddles was seconded from his job as Mechanical & Electrical Engineer for the LMS in Scotland, to work for the Ministry of Supply as Deputy Director General of Royal Engineer Equipment. By 1942, plans were in hand for the liberation of Western Europe, and locomotives capable of the steady haulage of heavy trains for long distances were needed. It had at first been envisaged that this need could be filled by Stanier's '8F' class 2-8-0, 240 of which were ordered from a variety of contractors, and many of these engines later performed their war service in the middle East. However, the '8F' had been designed in peacetime and a simpler machine was needed, capable of handling increased traffic at home as well as being suitable for work in continental Europe following a planned military breakthrough.

Below: The Keighley & Worth Valley Railway's policy is to recreate the country railway scene of the 1950s and this view is a timeless realisation of that aim: Riddles 'Standard' class 4MT 4-6-0 No. 75078 stands in the evening sun at Oxenhope, terminus of the five-mile branch line from Keighley with a train of BR liveried maroon rolling stock. This locomotive was rescued from Barry scrapyard in derelict condition in June 1972, and restored to working order by volunteers at Haworth.
Steve Le Cheminant.

Right: Riddles War Department 'Austerity' 2-8-0 No. 90595 awaits its next duty in the shed yard at Leeds Holbeck, on Thursday July 6 1961. The simple outline of the design is clearly apparent — note the unspoked disc bogie wheels, for example. Britain's only surviving 'WD' 2-8-0 can be found on the Worth Valley Railway — the locomotive was repatriated from Sweden in 1973. Although locomotives of this size were not normally expected to work tender-first, Riddles realised that this would be inevitable in time of war, and gave his 'Austerity' engines narrow coal bunkers, to permit good visibility from the cab when running in reverse. *Gavin Morrison.*

Below: The MHR's 'WD' 2-10-0 No. 90775 (a fictional number) at Ropley, on May 13 1986. Repatriated from Greece in 1984 with a further 2-10-0 and an American 'S160' 2-8-0, this locomotive provides an interesting comparison with its 2-8-0 predeccessor, with which it shared many common components, including wheels and motion. *Mick Roberts.*

In answer, Riddles produced his MoS 'Austerity' 2-8-0, which, although of roughly similar proportions to the Stanier 2-8-0, minimised use of steel castings, thereby obtaining worthwhile savings in scarce materials. The first example was handed over to the MoS by the North British Locomotive Company on January 16 1943, and the 2-8-0 was a machine of rugged simplicity: it was not, and was never intended to be, a masterpiece of aesthetic design, but it was by no means ugly either.

Riddles had produced exactly the right locomotive for the job in hand. It was powerful and versatile and could haul 1,000-ton trains on level track at speeds of around 40mph. Provision was made for the engine to work either with vacuum-braked trains (as in Britain) or air-braked stock. The class worked very successfully indeed in many different theatres of war: on Britain's railways and also in France, Belgium and Holland. After the war no fewer than 733 of these engines were taken into British stock, where many worked for another 20 years or so.

In common with many other classes, they became steadily less common after 1960, until by 1967 just 123 remained at work, in very work-weary condition. They were extinct as a working class by 1967 and none of the British engines were preserved, leaving a sad gap in Britain's collection of preserved locomotives. However, the volunteers of the Keighley & Worth Valley Railway were keen to see one of these historic machines back in the country of their origin and in 1973 repatriated No. 1931 from Sweden.

With the 2-8-0s in traffic during the war, Riddles enlarged the design into a 2-10-0 of similar appearance, for use over temporary, lightly-constructed tracks. Thus, while the 2-10-0 type weighed 78 tons cwt (locomotive only) against the 70 tons 10cwt of the 2-8-0, the larger engine's axle load was just $13\frac{1}{2}$ tons, compared with the 15.6 tons of the 2-8-0. The MoS 2-10-0s were built in the same economical way as their class 8 predecessors, including using the same wheels, cylinders and motion. They were the first locomotives with 10 coupled wheels to run successfully in this country, and thus paved the way for the brilliant class 9F Standard 2-10-0 introduced by Riddles for BR after Nationalisation.

The 150 MoS 2-10-0s were strong and capable, and after the war 25 examples were taken into British stock, these engines working mainly in Scotland. Numbered 90750-74 after 1948, the class was still intact in 1961, when the first withdrawals took place: all 25 engines were scrapped during 1962, and none of the former BR engines were preserved. Until the early 1980s, the only preserved MoS 2-10-0 in Britain was the blue-liveried *Gordon*, built in 1943 by the North British Locomotive Company. This locomotive was unusual in that it never worked overseas, spending its entire working life on the Longmoor Military Railway, in Hampshire, where members of the armed forces were trained in railway operations.Following closure of the LMR, *Gordon* was transferred on long-term loan to the Severn Valley Railway, where it is frequently seen in charge of heavy passenger trains.

For admirers of the Riddles 'Austerity' 2-10-0, until 1985 *Gordon* was the only working example and whilst bright and attractive to many visitors, the blue livery was perhaps not to the liking of the dedicated enthusiasts, who would have preferred to see one of these workaday engines in the plain, unlined black livery in which they used to be seen at work with seemingly endless coal trains. In these circumstances, the repatriation of a pair of these engines from Greece in 1984, a joint effort by the Mid Hants Railway and the Lavender Line, in Sussex, was well-received by British enthusiasts.

After the war, Riddles returned to full-time LMS service, but the war had left all four private companies in a regrettable state of disrepair, and there was little hope of catching up on the huge backlog of lost investment and maintenance. Furthermore, after the war, with a Labour Government in power, a broadly-based plan of social improvement was implemented: the welfare state was born and public utilities were taken into public ownership, the LMS, LNER, SR and GWR being welded into a single new unit, British Railways, at midnight on December 31 1947. On New Year's Day 1948, a new transport era began and the very different motive power fleets, requirements, and traditions of four very individual companies, which had frequently indulged in spirited competition, had to be welded into a single, coherent and workable whole. Thus, when Robert Riddles was appointed as CME of the new organisation, together with two of his former LMS colleagues, Roland C. Bond and E.S. Cox, in very senior motive power management positions, it was widely assumed that the new British Railways locomotive policy would carry a strong LMS flavour. Many senior officers of the former 'Big Four' companies — especially on the fiercely independent GWR — were deeply hostile to the state take-over; undoubtedly aware of the prevailing mood of uncertainty and suspicion, Riddles, Bond and Cox acted with care.

The day-to-day business of running the railway required a continuing supply of motive power, and this meant that around 400 new locomotives a year were needed, just to keep pace with the replacement of old and worn-out engines. Consequently, railway enthusiasts of whatever pre-nationalisation affiliation were delighted to see that after 1948 their favourite engines were still rolling out of the erecting shops at Swindon, Doncaster, Crewe and Eastleigh. But this was only an interim measure and Riddles and his men were already hard at work formulating a plan of campaign for the future. First of all, they had to decide whether they were going to continue with steam traction, pursue wide-scale electrification or introduce large numbers of main line diesel locomotives. At the time, any prospect of electrification had to be deferred and there was no money available for large-scale dieselisation, which would have required the import of large quantities of expensive fuel oil. The home-grown fuel — coal — might be of variable quality, but it was available in virtually unlimited amounts, and at a reasonable cost.

Riddles tackled the problem in two ways. First, E.S. Cox was charged with the task of drawing up preliminary specifications for a new range of locomotive classes, whilst at the same time Riddles organised the famous locomotive interchange trials of 1948. In these trials, of great interest to the enthusiast, various types of express, mixed traffic and and freight engine classes from all the former 'Big Four' groups were tested over the main lines of the other companies. Thus, LMS Stanier 'Black 5' and rebuilt 'Royal Scot' 4-6-0s ran on Southern metals, LNER 'A4' 4-6-2s ran on the LMS main line from Euston, Bulleid 'Pacifics' stormed the gradients of the Scottish Highlands in fine style and Collett's 'King' 4-6-0s worked into Leeds. A great deal of experience was gained, and the point was proved that a well-designed engine would work satisfactorily anywhere in the country, given a train within its capabilities and decent coal.

Perhaps BR should have recognised that steam was outmoded and moved towards more modern power, but finance was tight and it was made clear to Riddles, and Riddles made it clear to everyone else, that BR was investing in traction which gave the most motive power for every penny spent. At this time, diesel and electric traction was quite simply too expensive and whilst

Above: No. 70000 *Britannia*, built in 1951 at Crewe as the first of Robert Riddles range of new 'Standard' locomotives, a total of 999 engines which shared a strong family resemblance and simple, robust construction. *Britannia* was initially listed for official preservation, but sister locomotive No. 700013 *Oliver Cromwell* was substituted, leaving enthusiasts to rescue No. 70000. Based after withdrawal at the Severn Valley Railway and then the Nene Valley Railway, *Britannia* moved to Steamtown, Carnforth in December 1986 for major overhaul to main line running order.
W.A. Sharman.

in an ideal world modernisation should probably have followed, BR remained wedded to steam. Around 200 locomotive classes were inherited from the four groups, and these engines were of very different age, capability and usefulness. A decision was taken to produce new steam classes of Standard design, though various well-designed and proven features from pre-Nationalisation practice were incorporated into the new locomotives. The overall design work was supervised by Cox, who produced a commendable and attractive family appearance for the Standard classes.

By March 1949, overall specifications of the new range of locomotives had been finalised and detailed design work was distributed between the principal drawing offices of the four main groups, at Brighton, Swindon, Doncaster and Derby. In all, 12 classes were produced, including three 'Pacifics', two 4-6-0s, two 2-6-2Ts, three 2-6-0s, one 2-6-4T and one 2-10-0. With design work eventually complete, the main frames for the first of the new engines were laid down in the erecting shop at Crewe Works on December 3 1950 — and class 7P 'Pacific' No. 70000 *Britannia* was under way. As might be expected, this locomotive was 'launched' with much 'razamatazz' at Marylebone station, London, on January 30 1951, when Transport Minister Alfred Barnes unveiled the nameplate.

The former LMS drawing office at Derby supervised design work, all 55 'Britannias' were built at Crewe, and the class was complete by 1953. BR gave the class evocative names designed to strike a chord in the new Britain taking shape in the aftermath of the war, examples being: *William Shakespeare, Black Prince, Hotspur, Iron Duke, Polar Star, Rising Star, William Wordsworth, Robin Hood, Lord Kitchener, Anzac, Firh of Forth, Moray Firth.* Curiously, No. 70047 was never named. It was intended that the class could progressively take over the duties of engines like the 'Lord Nelson' and 'Royal Scot' 4-6-0s and the SR Bulleid 'Pacifics'. However, they prompted mixed reactions from footplate crews, for while they were capable engines, there was a good deal of uncomfortable vibration, and the cabs were noisy and very dusty, though efforts were subsequently made to rectify these difficulties. More serious were the mechanical problems in their early years, which prompted Riddles to withdraw the whole series from work when it was found that on seven members of the class the driving wheels had worked loose on their axles, resulting in bent motion rods. This fault was also rectified and the class went on to work very successfully, especially in East Anglia. The 'Britannias' had some novel features: the controls were carefully designed and grouped within reach of the seats provided on either side of the cab for the driver and the fireman, and the cab floor was cantilevered from the locomotive, providing an unbroken, flat surface to the front of the tender. Previously, the gap between engine and tender had generally been covered by a hinged plate, which could make life uncomfortable for the fireman. Some footplatemen never really got to like them however, especially on the Western Region, where it was felt that they fell far short of the GWR tradition, which was still a

Left: Unique Riddles class 8P 4-6-2 No. 71000 *Duke of Gloucester* crosses Swithland Viaduct, Great Central Railway with an 11-coach test train, on October 3 1986 following completion of its 12-year restoration from scrapyard condition. No. 71000 is carrying 'The Mid Day Scot' headboard. Although 'The Duke's boiler performance was disappointing, tests revealed the cylinders and machinery to be of unparalleled power and efficiency — but BR decided to terminate steam construction in favour of dieselisation before No. 71000's problems had been solved. *Mick Roberts.*

Left: A reminder of why many people even within the steam world believed that No. 71000 was an impossible restoration project. The locomotive is pictured here lying at Barry scrapyard in 1968, devoid of cylinders, pipework, valve gear and fittings. That such obstacles were overcome in such fine style is indeed a startling tribute to the determination and hard work of the Duke of Gloucester Steam Locomotive Trust Ltd. *Mike Pope.*

powerful force. Despite this, a batch of 'Britannia' class engines based at Cardiff Canton motive power depot did fine work on prestige trains such as 'The Red Dragon' express.

Most of the class succumbed to the oxy-acetylene cutting torch at Scottish scrapyards, the last-built engines having a working life of just 14 years — very short indeed for a main line steam locomotive. Had it not been for the implementation of the BR Modernisation Plan in 1955, after which new diesels were introduced at an ever-increasing rate, it is probable that the 'Britannias' would have been built in hundreds, rather than dozens. This is significant, for one criticism frequently levelled at the entire 'Standard' range was that there were never enough of them to reap the advantages of standardisation, but that they were built in sufficient numbers to further complicate the already difficult problem of the provision of spare parts on a nationwide basis.

Riddles also built a smaller version of the 'Britannia', using a similar chassis and wheels, fitted with a lighter boiler, producing a locomotive of greater route availability, lighter axle load, and slightly less power. Numbered in the sequence 72000-72009 and named after Scottish Clans, this class of engines worked mainly in Scotland, but were not regarded as particularly successful. Introduced in 1952 and also designed at Derby, the class was extinct by 1966 and none were

Above: Riddles class 9F 2-10-0 No. 92203 *Black Prince,* owned by wildlife artist David Shepherd and based on the East Somerset Railway at Cranmore, near Shepton Mallet, where it hauls passenger trains over the 2½-mile line to Mendip Vale. Robert Riddles based his entire range of Standard locomotives on the simple, coal-fired reciprocating steam engine, and as such *Black Prince* and *Evening Star* are direct descendants of Stephenson's *Rocket* of 1830. *Steve Le Cheminant.*

Right: This working reproduction of *Rocket,* constructed in 1979 for the National Railway Museum, was completed in time for the 150th anniversary in 1980 of the opening of the Liverpool & Manchester Railway. *Rocket,* which has travelled all over the world as an ambassador for the NRM, is seen here in steam at York in the snow outside the Museum, in January 1982. Although the cylinders subsequently moved from the rear of the locomotive to a position flanking the smokebox, the principles by which *Rocket* was propelled along the rails were exactly the same as those developed to such a fine degree in the Standard engines. *John Bellwood.*

preserved. This lack of conspicuous success also applied to Robert Riddles' third 'Pacific' built for BR, the unique class 8P No. 71000 *Duke of Gloucester*. However, whilst this locomotive was disappointing in traffic, it has become one of the shining triumphs of the preservation world, and knowledge gleaned during its restoration to working order has shown that some of its shortcomings in service may not have been a consequence of poor design, but mistakes made during construction. *Duke of Gloucester* was intended to be the culmination of more than 100 years experience of steam locomotive design, construction and operation, a machine of superb efficiency and power — and in appearance at least it certainly 'looked the part'. By June 1954 the new engine was at work on the West Coast Main Line, where it was rostered for regular turns of duty on the 'Mid Day Scot' express. But all was not well with 'The Duke' which was unpredictable and disappointing both in service and during controlled, scientific testing, giving particular trouble when there was a continuous, high demand for steam — the boiler did not seem able to keep pace with the demands of the cylinders at high output. Various modifications were tried, with limited success, but whilst various high-ranking BR officers, including Riddles and Cox, wanted to identify the reasons for the poor performance of the 'Duke's' boiler they were overtaken by events, when the decision was taken to terminate steam construction in favour of dieselisation.

No longer required after just eight years in existence, No. 71000 was initially listed for official preservation, but perhaps as a result of its tarnished image and disappointing performance, plans were changed and a decision was taken to preserve only the most successful parts of the locomotive. In 1967, the left-hand valve gear and cylinder was removed, sectioned and placed on display in the Science Museum, in South Kensington, London. The other cylinder was also subsequently removed and the dismembered hulk of the unique locomotive was then sold to Dai Woodham, of Barry, for scrap, the 4-6-2 duly taking its place in the rows of rusty engines. The locomotive was judged to be beyond economic repair, but a group of enthusiasts in the East Midlands believed otherwise and undeterred by the incomplete nature of the locomotive, which had also lost its tender, pressed ahead with their fund raising activities.

They succeeeded in their aim and eventually bought No. 71000, which was transported in 1973 to the Loughborough headquarters of the Great Central Railway, where the long and very expensive business of restoration began. There were those even within the steam business, fully accustomed to the difficulties of the restoration of scrapyard steam engines, who shook their heads in disbelief at the enormously complex task facing the Duke of Gloucester Steam

Locomotive Trust Ltd. The small group of enthusiasts laboured on regardless, working at weekends and during holidays, scraping, cleaning and refurbishing the parts they had, and scrimping and saving to buy those they didn't possess. The most expensive parts were the new cylinders and full set of connecting rods, coupling rods, rotary drive shafts and complex geared cam-boxes which comprise the distinctive Caprotti valve gear. Money was raised, industrial concerns were persuaded to give their services at bargain rates or even free of charge and slowly, very slowly, the 'Duke' started to take shape once again. But it was an agonisingly slow process which in total occupied 12 years of hard effort.

Of course, No. 71000 was a 'one-off' and in the context of everyday service, a rare locomotive of questionable usefulness. The remaining 998 engines built to the Standard designs of Robert Riddles fulfilled a useful function and worked in all corners of the British network. Of the 12 designs which saw service, four are not represented in preservation, these being the 'Clan' 4-6-2s of the 72xxx series, the class 3 2-6-0s of the 77xxx series, the class 2 2-6-2Ts of the 84xxx series and the class 3 2-6-2Ts of the 82xxx sequence. However, members of the other eight classes do survive for us to enjoy and study today at a variety of locations around the country.

The largest and in many ways most impressive of the successful Riddles classes was the masterful class 9F 2-10-0, of which 251 examples were built at Crewe and Swindon between 1953 and 1960. Known to many enthusiasts as 'Spaceships' for their (then) very modern appearance, they were extremely powerful and whilst designed for freight haulage, nevertheless carried out a percentage of passenger mileage, some at extremely high speed for a freight design.

For example, in July 1958, the Eastern Region's No. 92184, called to haul the up 'Flying Scotsman' because of an engine failure, hurtled down Stoke Bank (scene of *Mallard's* famous 126mph sprint of 1938) at 90mph, at which speed the 5ft diameter coupled wheels would be spinning at 500 revolutions per minute — or nearly $8\frac{1}{2}$ times per second! Such high speed running was not popular with the BR authorities and operators were ordered not to use the '9Fs' in this way. Even so, spectacular incidents continued to be reported, the most famous of these concerning the running of the top link 'Red Dragon' and 'Capitals United' expresses from South Wales to Paddington.

In 1960, No. 92220 *Evening Star*, based at Cardiff Canton engine shed, was kept in pristine condition as the shed 'flagship'. Thus, when the rostered 'Britannia' for the 'Red Dragon' of June 27 that year failed, *Evening Star* deputised and successfully completed the return trip to London. With 13 coaches weighing 450 tons behind the tender, *Evening Star* performed with considerable style, burning less coal than a 'Britannia' 4-6-2 or GWR 'Castle' 4-6-0 would be expected to use on the same duty, and running at maximum speeds of 85mph! The shed staff and footplatemen were clearly impressed by this sparkling performance and four further similar express duties were worked by *Evening Star* before curt, but very clear orders from above called a halt. But the men of Canton shed had revealed with great style what superb engines the Riddles '9Fs' were!

The first '9F' withdrawals occurred in 1964 and by the end of 1966 half the engines had been scrapped; by 1968, the last year of everyday steam traction on BR metals, just 17 examples remained in service. No. 92220 *Evening Star*, in common with many sister engines, was withdrawn after just five years at work, in March 1965 and was stored in various locations prior to taking up a permanent home at the National Railway Museum. The locomotive was restored in spring 1967 at Crewe Works, where so many of the class had been built.

Riddles and his team had incorporated into the Standard classes various useful design features developed by the four companies of the pre-1948 years. However, some of the Riddles engines had rather more direct connections with pre-Nationalisation locomotives. For example, the Standard Class 5 mixed traffic 4-6-0, in the 73xxx number series, was a thinly disguised version of the ubiquitous Stanier Class 5MT 4-6-0, built in such huge numbers by both the LMS and BR (See Chapter 5). The Standard '5' displayed the clean and distinctive family resemblance which Cox gave all the Standard classes, but in its essential proportions it was a 'Black 5'. As such the '73xxx' series locomotives were versatile, capable and popular amongst footplatemen of the 1950s and 1960s and the class of 172 examples worked in many parts of Britain. Two groups of engines were given names associated with the Arthurian legends, including: Nos. 73080 *Merlin*, 73081 *Excalibur* and 73110 *The Red Knight*. The first of the class appeared in April 1951, but in common with other Standard types, had uneconomically short lives. The first withdrawals occurred in 1964 and within two years more than half had been scrapped. The final example, No. 73069, worked at Carnforth to the very end of steam operation, in August 1968. As with the Stanier 'Black 5s', versatility was a hallmark of the class and they worked all types of trains from fast expresses to humble pick-up goods duties. The Standard Class 5s were well suited to the rough-and-tumble of service in the 1950s and 1960s, and in the early 1980s admirers of these engines could see only one example at work, No. 73050 *City of Peterborough* (not a name carried in service) on the Nene Valley Railway, near Peterborough.

Three other Riddles classes also modelled on existing LMS designs were the class 4 2-6-0s of the 76xxx series, the class 4 2-6-4Ts of the 80xxx series, and the class 2 2-6-0s of the 78xxx series. For example, the class 4 mixed traffic 2-6-0s were very similar to the Ivatt class 4MT 2-6-0s of the 43000 series, introduced in 1947 and represented in preservation by No. 43106, on the Severn Valley Railway. The Riddles version of this class of 115 engines are represented in the 1980s by four survivors, of which only one was back at work by 1987, No. 76017 on the Mid Hants Railway. No. 76017 was built in July 1953 and withdrawn in July 1965, after which the locomotive was despatched to Barry. The 2-6-0 was bought by the Standard 4 Preservation Group and moved to the Quanton Railway Centre, Buckinghamshire, in January 1974, and was subsequently transferred to the MHR, where restoration was completed.

The BR Standard locomotives were simple, robust, easy and cheap to maintain, aalthough they were not initially well-received in many quarters either by footplatemen or lineside observers, as they were seen as displacing favourite pre-Nationalisation types and classes. Political will changed, 'the goalposts were moved' and steam construction was stopped before the Standard classes could make much of an impact. If determined attempts had been made to resolve the indifferent boiler performance of No. 71000 *Duke of Gloucester* — and testing in the 1950s had indicated that its chassis and cylinders were of unparalleled efficiency and high-power — then a class of production locomotives might have followed as a worthy advance on the achievements of Gresley and Stanier. As it was, while the 'Britannias' did well on many passenger turns, the prestige duties of the four main groups during the 1950s, remained in the charge of Collett's 'Kings' and 'Castles', Stanier's magnificent 'Princess Coronation' and 'Princess Royal' class 'Pacifics', Gresley's superb 'A3' and 'A4' 'Pacifics' and Bulleid's controversial 'Merchant Navy', 'West Country' and 'Battle of Britain' class 'Pacifics' , in both original and modified forms. The Standard designs of Robert Riddles and his team, in retrospect, can be seen as well-designed and capable prime movers ideally suited to the busy railway of the period. It is heartening to record that so many survive — at least they will now experience a working life of reasonable length!

CHAPTER 9:
LOCOMOTIVE STOCKLIST

THIS chapter lists the steam locomotives which survive today from the former 'Big Four' companies of the pre-Nationalisation era together with those built by British Railways after 1948, to the design of Robert Riddles. Brief details are also provided of where they could be seen, at the time of going to press.

The locomotives are grouped in ascending order of their post-1948 British Railways number sequences, starting with the locomotives of the former GWR, and continuing with those of the SR, LMS, LNER and concluding with the BR locomotives. Pre-Nationalisation numbers are also given. Each heading (in bold type) gives details of the class of locomotive and its wheel arrangement, together with an indication, where appropriate, of pre-Grouping (pre-1923) origins and the name of the designer. Locomotive names are given in italics, and the initials of the private railways where they may be seen today are to be found in the right hand column, in light italics. Keys are provided to identify the historic railway names given in the headings, and also the private railways of today.

This chapter contains details only of the preserved steam locomotives formerly owned by the former 'Big Four' companies or BR — it does not include any of the preserved industrial shunting locomotives, of which there are also about 550 examples, accompanying their bigger shed-mates, scattered around the country at museums, steam centres or private railways. The voluntary supporting associations or operating authorities of most private steam railways are members of the Association of Railway Preservation Societies, which can provide details of its members for anyone wishing to become involved in railway preservation, either as an active working member, or as an 'armchair' supporter. The ARPS, in conjunction with BP Oil Ltd., publishes a free annual leaflet giving brief details of the location of operating railways, museums and steam centres, together with an indication of the numbers of locomotives, carriages and also the public facilities available at each location. This useful leaflet is available free of charge from the ARPS, 3 Orchard Close, Watford, Herts, England, WD1 3DU — but please remember to enclose a 9in × 4in stamped self-addressed envelope.

All information for this chapter was kindly provided by Platform 5 Publishing Ltd., of Sheffield, whose 'Preserved Locomotives and Multiple Units' which

gives full and comprehensive historic and statistical details of the locomotives listed here, is published approximately every 18 months.

Above: BR Class 4MT 2-6-4T No. 80064 crosses Maypool Viaduct on the Torbay & Dartmouth Steam Railway on September 12 1982, with the 1700 Kingswear-Paignton service. This locomotive is now based on the Bluebell Railway. *Mark Wilkins.*

GREAT WESTERN RAILWAY

Taff Vale Railway 0-6-2T (Class 02)
85/426 .... *KWVR*

Taff Vale Railway 0-6-2T (Class 01)
28/450 .... *CRS*

Port Talbot Railway 0-6-0ST
26/813 .... *SVR*

Powlesland & Mason 0-4-0ST
6/921 .... *Leicester Museum of Technology*

Cardiff Railway 0-4-0ST
1338 .... *Somerset Railway Museum*

Alexandra Docks & Rly Co 0-4-0ST
1340 *Trojan* .... *DRC*

GWR 0-6-0ST (Churchward, Class '1361')
1363 .... *DRC*

GWR 0-6-0PT (Collett, Class '1366')
1369 .... *DVR*

North Pembrokeshire & Fishguard Rlys 0-6-0ST
2/1378 *Margaret* .... *SMM*

GWR 0-4-2T (Collett, Class '14xx')
4820/1420 *Bulliver* .... *DVR*
4842/1442 .... *Tiverton Museum.*
4850/1450 *Ashburton* .... *DVR*
4866/1466 .... *DRC*

GWR 0-6-0PT (Hawksworth, Class '15xx')
1501 .... *SVR*

GWR 0-6-0PT (Hawksworth, Class '16xx')
1638 *Dartington* .... *DVR*

GWR 0-6-0 (Collett, Class '2251')
3205 .... *SVR*

GWR 'Dean Goods' 0-6-0 (Dean, Class '2301')
2516 .... *GWM*

HISTORIC RAILWAY COMPANY KEY

BR	British Railways
CR	Caledonian Railway
FR	Furness Railways
GCR	Great Central Railway
GER	Great Eastern Railway
GJR	Grand Junction Railway
GNR	Great Northern Railway
GNSR	Great North of Scotland Railway
GSWR	Glasgow & South Western Railway
GWR	Great Western Railway
HR	Highland Railway
LBSCR	London Brighton & South Coast Railway
LMR	Liverpool & Manchester Railway
LMS	London Midland & Scottish Railway
LNER	London & North Eastern Railway
LNWR	London & North Western Railway
LSWR	London & South Western Railway
LTSR	London Tilbury & Southend Railway
LYR	Lancashire & Yorkshire Railway
MR	Midland Railway
NBR	North British Railway
NER	North Eastern Railway
NLR	North London Railway
NSR	North Staffordshire Railway
SDR	Stockton & Darlington Railway
SDJR	Somerset & Dorset Joint Railway
SECR	South Eastern & Chatham Railway
SR	Southern Railway
WD	War Department

PRESERVED RAILWAY KEY

BI .... Barry Island (Scrapyard, not open to the public).

BKR ... Bo'ness & Kinneil Railway, Bo'ness, West Lothian.

BR .... Bluebell Railway, West Sussex.

BRC . Buckinghamshire Railway Centre, Quainton, Buckinghamshire.

BRCH ..... Bulmer Railway Centre, Herefordshire.

BRM ...... Birmingham Railway Museum, Tyseley.

BSM ...... Bressingham Steam Museum, Nr. Diss, Norfolk.

BSR . Bristol Suburban Railway, Bitton, Nr. Bristol.

BWR .... Bodmin & Wenford Railway, Cornwall.

COLM .... City of Liverpool Museum.

CRS .. Caerphilly Railway Society, Caerphilly, Mid Glamorgan.

CVR . Colne Valley Railway, Nr. Colchester, Essex.

CWMM ...... Chatterley Whitfield Mining Museum, Derbyshire.

CWR . Chosley & Wallingford Railway, Wallingford, Oxfordshire.

DFR .... Dean Forest Railway, Norchard, Gloucestershire.

DR . Dinting Railway Centre, Glossop, Derbyshire.

DNRM .... Darlington North Road Museum.

DRC . Didcot Railway Centre, Didcot, Oxfordshire.

DVR ... Dart Valley Railway, Buckfastleigh, Devon.

ELR .. East Lancashire Railway, Bury, Lancashire.

ESR .... East Somerset Railway, Cranmore, Somerset.

FLC ... Fleetwood Locomotive Centre, Fleetwood, Lancashire.

GCR .... Great Central Railway, Loughborough, Leicestershire.

GMSI .. Greater Manchester Museum of Science & Industry, Manchester.

GWM .. Great Western Railway Museum, Swindon, Wiltshire.

HSTT . Horsehay Steam Trust, Telford, Shropshire.

HLPG ...... Humberside Locomotive Preservation Group, Hull.

IoW .... Isle of Wight Steam Railway, Isle of Wight, Hampshire.

KESR ... Kent & East Sussex Railway, Tenterden, Kent

KWVR Keighley & Worth Valley Railway, Keighley, West Yorkshire.

LHR .... Lakeside & Haverthwaite Railway, Nr. Ulverston, Cumbria.

LMPM .... Lytham Motive Power Museum.

LR .... Llangollen Railway, Llangollen, Clwyd.

LSVR ... Lower Swansea Valley Railway, Swansea, Glamorgan.

MHR .... Mid Hants Railway, Alresford, Hampshire.

MR .... Middleton Railway, Leeds, Yorkshire.

MRC .... Midland Railway Centre, Nr. Ripley, Derbyshire.

NNR . North Norfolk Railway, Sheringham, Norfolk.

NRM .... National Railway Museum, York.

NSR .... North Staffordshire Railway, Cheddleton, Staffordshire.

NVR .... Nene Valley Railway, Wansford, Nr. Peterborough, Cambridgeshire.

NWSM .... North Woolwich Station Museum.

NYMR . North Yorkshire Moors Railway, Pickering, North Yorkshire.

PR .... Peak Rail, Buxton, Derbyshire.

PVR .... Plym Valley Railway, Plymouth, Devon.

SCR .. Swindon & Cricklade Railway, Nr. Swindon, Wiltshire.

SMM .... Scolton Manor Museum, Dyfed.

SR .... Strathspey Railway, Boat of Garten, Highlands.

SRC .... Southall Railway Centre, Middlesex.

SRM ...... Steamport Railway Museum, Southport, Lancashire.

SRPS ...... Scottish Railway Preservation Society, Falkirk, Central Region.

STVR Stour Valley Railway, Nr. Colchester, Essex.

S'TWN .. Steamtown Railway Museum, Carnforth, Lancashire.

SVR .... Severn Valley Railway, Bridgnorth, Shropshire.

SW .... Swanage Railway, Swanage, Dorset.

TOD ...... Gloucestershire Warwickshire Railway.

TDSR .... Torbay & Dartmouth Steam Railway, Paignton, Devon.

TVRS ... Taff Vale Railway Society, Merthyr Tydfil, Mid Glamorgan.

WSR .... West Somerset Railway, Minehead, Somerset.

GWR 2-8-0 (Churchward Class '28xx')
2807	TOD
2818	NRM
2857	SVR
2859	BI
2861	BI
2873	BI
2874	BI
2885	SRC
3802	PVR
3803	DVR
3814	NYMR
3822	DRC
3845	BI
3850	WSR
3855	BI
3862	BI

'Dukedog' 4-4-0 (Collett, Class '90xx')
9017/3217 Earl of Berkeley	BR

'City' 4-4-0 (Churchward, Class '37xx')
3717/3440 City of Truro	NRM

'Star' 4-6-0 (Churchward, Class '40xx')
4003 Lode Star	GWM

'Castle' 4-6-0 (Collett, Class '4073')
4073 Caerphilly Castle	Science Museum
5029 Nunney Castle	DRC
5043 Earl of Mount Edgcumbe	BRM
5051 Drysllwyn Castle	DRC
5080 Defiant	BRM
7027 Thornbury Castle	BRM
7029 Clun Castle	BRM

GWR 2-8-0T (Churchward, Class '42xx')
4247	CWR
4248	Shipyard Services, Essex
4253	BI
4270	LSVR
4277	TOD

GWR 2-6-0 (Churchward, Class '43xx')
5322/8322	DRC
7325/9303	SVR

GWR 2-6-2T (Churchward, Class '45xx')
4555	TDSR
4561	WSR
4566	SVR
4588	DVR
5521	DFR
5526	TOD
5532	DFR
5538	BI
5539	BI
5541	DFR
5542	WSR
5552	BWR
5553	BI
5972	DRC

'Hall' 4-6-0 (Collett, Class '49xx')
4920 Dumbleton Hall	DVR
4930 Hagley Hall	SVR
4936 Kinlet Hall	TOD
4942 Maindy Hall	DRC
4953 Pitchford Hall	DFR
4979 Wootton Hall	FLC
4983 Albert Hall	BRM
5900 Hinderton Hall	DRC
5952 Cogan Hall	TOD
5967 Bickmarsh Hall	BI
5972 Olton Hall	Procor Ltd., Wakefield

GWR 2-6-2T (Collett, Class '5101')
4110	SRC
4115	BI
4121	DFR
4141	SVR
4144	DRC
4150	SVR
4160	PVR
5164	SVR
5193	SRM
5199	TOD

GWR 2-8-0T (Collett, Class '5205')
5224	GCR
5227	BI
5239 Goliath	TDSR

GWR 0-6-2T (Collett, Class '56xx')
5619	HSTT
5637	SCR
5643	S'TWN
5668	TVRS
6619	NYMR
6634	ESR
6686	BI
6695	SW
6697	DRC

GWR 0-6-0PT (Collett, Class '57xx')
3650	DRC
3738	DRC
4612	KWVR
5764	SVR
5775	KWVR
5786	BRCH
7714	SVR
7715	BRC
7752	BRM
7754	LR
7760	BRM
9600	BRM
9629	Cardiff Holiday Inn
9642	BP Chemicals, Baglan Bay
9681	DFR
9682	SRC

GWR 'King' 4-6-0 (Collett, Class '60xx')
6000 King George V	BRCH
6023 King Edward II	Bristol Temple Meads Station
6024 King Edward I	BRC

GWR 2-6-2T (Collett, Class '61xx')
6106	DRC

GWR 0-6-0PT (Collett, Class '64xx')
6412	WSR
6430/35	DVR

GWR 'Modified Hall' 4-6-0 (Hawksworth, Class '6959')
6960 Raveningham Hall	SVR
6984 Owsden Hall	Bicester Timber Yard
6989 Wightwick Hall	BRC
6990 Witherslack Hall	GCR

6998 *Burton Agnes Hall* .... DRC
7903 *Foremark Hall* .... SCR
7927 *Willington Hall* .... BI

GWR 2-8-2T (Collett, Class '72xx')
7200 .... BRC
7202 .... DRC
7229 .... PVR

GWR 'Manor' 4-6-0 (Collett, Class '78xx')
7802 *Bradley Manor* .... SVR
7808 *Cookham Manor* .... DRC
7812 *Erlestoke Manor* .... SVR
7819 *Hinton Manor* .... SVR
7820 *Dinmore Manor* .... WSR
7821 *Ditcheat Manor* .... TOD
7822 *Foxcote Manor* .... LR
7827 *Lydham Manor* .... TDSR
7828 *Odney Manor* .... TOD

GWR 0-6-0PT (Hawksworth, Class '94xx')
9400 .... GWM
9466 .... BRC

Shropshire & Montgomery Rly 0-4-2WT
1 *Gazelle* .... *Museum of Army Transport, Beverley*

Burry Port & Gwendraeth Valley Rly 0-6-0ST
2 *Pontyberem* .... DRC

Sandy & Potton Rly 0-4-0WT
5/1863 *Shannon* .... DRC

South Devon Rly 0-4-0WT (7ft gauge)
151/2180 *Tiny* .... DVR

SOUTHERN RAILWAY

LSWR 0-4-4T (Adams, Class 02)
E209-W24/W24 *Calbourne* .... IoW

LSWR 0-4-4T (Drummond, Class 'M7')
E53-53/30053 .... SW
E245-245/30245 .... NRM

Class USA 0-6-0T
64/30064 .... BR
65/30065 *Maunsell* .... KESR
70/30070 *Wainwright* .... KESR
72/30072 .... KWVR

LSWR 0-4-0T (Adams, Class B4)
E96-96/30096 *Normandy* .... BR
E102-102/30102 *Granville* .... BSM

LSWR 4-4-0 (Drummond, Class T9)
E120-120/30120 .... MHR

LSWR 4-6-0 (Urie, Class S15)
E499-499/30499 .... MHR
E506-506/30506 .... MHR

SR 0-6-0 (Maunsell, Class Q)
541/30541 .... BR

LSWR 4-4-2T (Adams, Class 0415)
E0488-3488/30583 .... BR

LSWR 2-4-0WT (Beattie, Class 0298)
E0314-3314/30585 .... BRC
E0298-3298/30587 .... DVR

SR 'King Arthur' 4-6-0 (Maunsell, Class N15)
777/30777 *Sir Lamiel* .... HLPG

SR 4-6-0 (Maunsell, Class S15)
825/30825 .... *Shipyard Services, Essex*
828/30828 .... *Eastleigh Works, BREL*
830/30830 .... BI
841/30841 .... NYMR
847/30847 .... BR

SR 'Lord Nelson' 4-6-0 (Maunsell, Class 'LN')
E850-850/30850 *Lord Nelson* .... S'TWN

SR 'Schools' 4-4-0 (Maunsell, Class V)
925/30925 *Cheltenham* .... NRM
928/30928 *Stowe* .... BR

SECR 0-6-0T (Wainwright, Class P)
A27-1027/31027 .... BR
A178-1178/31178 .... BR
A323-1323/31323 .... BR
A556-1556/31556 .... KESR

SECR 0-6-0 (Wainwright, Class 01)
A65-1065/31065 .... *Sellinge*

SECR 0-4-4T (Wainwright, Class H)
A263-1263/31263 .... BR

SECR 0-6-0 (Wainwright, Class C)
A592-1592/31592-DS239 .... BR

SR 2-6-0 (Maunsell, Class U)
A618-1618/31618 .... BR
A625-1625/31625 .... MHR
A638-1638/31638 .... BR
A806-1806/31806 .... MHR

SECR 4-4-0 (Wainwright, Class D)
A737-1737/31737 .... NRM

SECR 2-6-0 (Maunsell, Class N)
A874-1874/31874 *Brian Fisk* .... MHR

LBSCR 0-6-0T (Stroudley, Class E1)
B110/32110 .... ESR

LBSCR 0-6-2T (Billinton, Class E4)
B473-2473/32473 *Birch Grove* .... BR

LBSCR 'Terrier' 0-6-0T (Stroudley, Class A1 & A1X)
B636-2636/32636 *Fenchurch* .... BR
W11-2640/32640 *Newport* .... IoW
W2-W8/32646 *Freshwater* .... IoW
B650-W9/32650 *Whitechapel* .... KESR
B655-2655/32655 *Stepney* .... BR
B662-2662/32662 *Martello* .... BSM
32670 *Poplar* .... KESR
B678-W-4-W/32678 *Knowle* .... *Woolwich*
380S *Boxhill* .... NRM

SR 0-6-0 (Bulleid, Class Q1)
C1/33001 .... BR

SR 'West Country' and 'Battle of Britain' 4-6-2 (Bulleid, Class WC & BB)
21C107/34007 *Wadebridge* .... PVR
21C110/34010 *Sidmouth* .... NYMR
21C116/34016 *Bodmin* .... MHR
21C123/34023 *Blackmore Vale* .... BR
21C127/34027 *Taw Valley* .... SVR
21C128/34028 *Eddystone* . *SR Pacific Group, Sellinge*
21C139/34039 *Boscastle* .... GCR
21C146/34046 *Braunton* .... BI
21C151/34051 *Winston Churchill* .... NRM
21C153/34053 *Sir Keith Park* .... HLPG
21C158/34058 *Sir Frederick Pile* .... BSR
21C159/34059 *Sir Archibald Sinclair* .... BR
21C167/34067 *Tangmere* .... MHR
21C170/34070 *Manston* .... *Richborough, Kent*
34072 *257 Squadron* .... SCR
34073 *249 Squadron* .... BI
34081 *92 Squadron* .... NVR
34092 *City of Wells* .... KWVR
34101 *Hartland* .... *Shaws Metal Supplies, Derby*
34105 *Swanage* .... MHR

'Merchant Navy' 4-6-2 (Bulleid, Class MN)
21C5/35005 *Canadian Pacific* .... S'TWN
21C6/35006 *Peninsular & Orient Steam Navigation Co* .... TOD
21C9/35009 *Shaw Savill* .... BI
21C10/35010 *Blue Star* .... *Victoria Dock, London*
21C11/35011 *General Steam Navigation* .... BI
21C18/35018 *British India Line* .... MHR
35022 *Holland America Line* .... SW
35025 *Brocklebank Line* .... GCR
35027 *Port Line* .... SCR
35028 *Clan Line* .... *Marylebone/Southall*
35029 *Ellerman Lines* .... NRM

LSWR 4-4-0 (Adams, Class T3)
563/E563 .... NRM

LBSCR 'Gladstone' 0-4-2 (Stroudley, Class B1)
214-618/B618 *Gladstone* .... NRM
Canterbury and Whitstable Rly 0-4-0
Invicta .... *Poor Priest Hospital, Canterbury*

LONDON MIDLAND AND SCOTTISH RAILWAY

MR 'Compound' 4-4-0 (Johnson, Class 4P)
1000/41000 .... NRM

LMS 2-6-2T (Ivatt, Class 2MT)
41241 .... KWVR
41298 .... BRC
41312 .... CRS
41313 .... BRC

MR 0-6-0T (Johnson, Class 1F)
1708/41708 .... MRC

LTSR 4-4-2T (Whitelegg, Class 3P)
2148/41966 *Thundersley* .... BSM

LMS Design 2-6-4T (Fairburn, Class 4MT)
42073 .... LHR
42085 .... LHR

LMS 2-6-4T (Stanier, Class 4MT)
2500/42500 .... BSM

LMS 'Crab' 2-6-0 (Hughes-Fowler, Class 5MT)
13000-2700/42700 .... NRM
13065-2765/42765 .... KWVR
13159-2859/42859 .... HLPG

LMS 2-6-0 (Stanier, Class 5MT)
13268-2968/42968 .... SVR

LMS 2-6-0 (Ivatt, Class 4MT)
43106 .... SVR

MR 0-6-0 (Fowler, Class 4F)
3942/43924 .... KWVR
4027/44027 .... MRC
4123/44123 .... BSR
4422/44422 .... NSR

LMS 'Black Five' 4-6-0 (Stanier, Class 5MT)
4767/44767 *George Stephenson* .... NYMR
4806/44806 *Magpie* .... GMSI
4871/44871 *Sovereign* .... S'TWN
4901/44901 .... BI
4932/44932 .... MRC
5000/45000 .... SVR
5025/45025 .... SR
5110/45110 *RAF Biggin Hill* .... SVR
5163/45163 .... HLPG
5212/45212 .... KWVR
5231/45231 *3rd (Volunteer) Battalion of the Worcestershire and Sherwood Foresters Regiment* .... GCR
5293/45293 .... *Victoria Dock, London*
5305/45305 .... HLPG
5337/45337 .... ELR
5379/45379 .... BSR
5407/45407 .... S'TWN
5428/45428 *Eric Treacy* .... NYMR
5491/45491 .... FLC

LMS 'Jubilee' 4-6-0 (Stanier, Class 6P, Formerly 5XP)
5593/45593 *Kolhapur* .... BRM
5596/45596 *Bahamas* .... DRC
5690/45690 *Leander* .... SVR
5699/45699 *Galatea* .... SVR

LMS 'Royal Scot' 4-6-0 (Fowler, Class 7P, formerly 6P)
6100/46100 *Royal Scot* .... BSM
6115/46115 *Scots Guardsman* .... DR

LMS 'Princess Royal' 4-6-2 (Stanier, Class 8P, formerly 7P)
6201/46201 *Princess Elizabeth* .... BRC
6203/46203 *Princess Margaret Rose* .... MRC

LMS 'Princess Coronation' 4-6-2 (Stanier, Class 8P, formerly 7P)
6229/46229 *Duchess of Hamilton* .... NRM
6233/46233 *Duchess of Sutherland* .... BSM
6235/46235 *City of Birmingham* . *Birmingham Science Museum*

LMS 2-6-0 (Ivatt, Class 2MT)
46428 .... SR
46441 .... S'TWN
46443 .... SVR
46447 .... BRC
46464 .... SR
46512 .... SR
46521 .... SVR

LMS 'Jinty' 0-6-0T (Fowler, Class 3F)
7119-7279/47279 .... KWVR
7138-7298/47298 .... LR
16407-7324/47324 .... BSR
16410-7327/47327 .... MRC
16440-7357/47357 .... MRC
16466-7383/47383 .... SVR
16489-7406/47406 .... PR
16528-7445/47445 .... MRC
16576-7493/47493 .... ESR
16647-7564/47564 .... MRC

LMS 2-8-0 (Stanier, Class 8F)
8151/48151 .... *Dewsbury*
8173/48173 .... BI
8305/48305 .... GCR
8431/48431 .... KWVR
48518 .... BI

48624 .... PR
8233/48773 .... SVR

LNWR 0-8-0 (Beames, Class 7F)
9395/49395 .... Blists Hill Open Air Museum

LYR 2-4-2T (Aspinall, Class 2P)
10621/50621 .... NRM

LYR 'Pug' 0-4-0ST (Aspinall, Class '0F')
11218/51218 .... KWVR
19 .... KWVR

LYR 0-6-0ST (Barton Wright, Class '2F')
752/11456 .... KWVR

LYR 'Ironclad' 0-6-0 (Barton Wright, Class '2F')
12044/52044 .... KWVR

LYR 0-6-0 (Aspinall, Class 3F)
1300/12322/52322 .... S'TWN

S&DJR 2-8-0 (Fowler, Class '7F')
9678-13808/53808 .... WSR
9679-13809/53809 .... MRC

CR 4-2-2 (Drummond, Class '1P')
14010/123 .... Glasgow Transport Museum

CR 0-4-4T (McIntosh, Class '439')
15189/55189 .... BKR

GSWR 0-6-0T (Drummond, Class '322')
916379 .... Glasgow Transport Museum

CR 0-6-0 (McIntosh, Class '812')
17566/57566 .... SR

HR 'Jones Goods' 4-6-0
103/17916 .... Glasgow Transport Museum

NLR 0-6-0T (Park, Class '75')
7505/58850 .... BR

LNWR 'Coal Tank' 0-6-2T (Webb, Class 'LNWR')
1054/7799/58926 .... DR

MR 2-4-0 (Kirtley, Class '1P')
158-158A/2-20002 .... MRC

MR 'Spinner' 4-2-2 (Johnson, Class 'IP')
118-673/673 .... NRM

NSR 0-6-2T (Hookham, Class 'New L')
2/2271 .... CWMM

LNWR 'Precedent' 2-4-0 (Webb)
790/5031 Hardwicke .... NRM

LNWR 2-2-2 (Ramsbottom)
173-3020 Cornwall .... NRM

LNWR 0-4-0ST (Ramsbottom)
1439/3042 .... NRM

GJR 2-2-2 (Trevithick)
49 Columbine .... NRM

FR 0-4-0
3 Coppernob .... NRM

FR 0-4-0ST
18 Chloe .... S'TWN
25/17 .... S'TWN

L&MR 0-2-2
Rocket .... Science Museum

L&MR 0-4-2
116/57 Lion .... COLM

L&MR 0-4-0
Sans Pareil .... SM

Mersey Rly 0-6-4T
5 Cecil Raikes .... SRM

LONDON AND NORTH EASTERN RLY

LNER 4-6-2 (Gresley, Class A4)
4498-7/60007 Sir Nigel Gresley .... Marylebone
4488-9/60069 Union of South Africa ....
.... Markinch Goods Depot, Fife
4464-19/60019 Bittern .... ICI Wilton, Middlesborough
4468-22/60022 Mallard .... NRM

LNER 4-6-2- (Gresley, Class A3)
1472-4472/60103 Flying Scotsman .... S'TWN/
Marylebone

LNER 4-6-2 (Peppercorn, Class A2)
60532 Blue Peter .... ICI Wilton, Middlesborough

LNER 2-6-2 (Gresley, Class V2)
4771/60800 Green Arrow .... NRM

LNER 4-6-0 (Thompson, Class B1)
1264/61264 .... GCR
1306/61306 Mayflower .... GCR

GER 4-6-0 (Holden, Class B12)
8572/61572 .... NNR

LNER 2-6-0 (Gresley, Class K4)
3442/61994 The Great Marquess .... SVR

LNER 2-6-0 (Peppercorn, Class K1)
2005/62005 .... NYMR

GNSR 4-4-0 (Pickersgill, Class D40)
49/6849-2277/62277 Gordon Highlander .... GTM

NBR 'Glen' 4-4-0 (Reid, Class D34)
256/9256-2469/62469 Glen Douglas .... GTM

GCR 'Improved Director' 4-4-0 (Robinson, Class D11)
506/5506-2660/62660 Butler Henderson .... GCR

LNER 4-4-0 (Gresley, Class D49)
246-2712/62712 Morayshire .... SRPS

GER 2-4-0 (Holden, Class E4)
7490-2785/62785 .... BSM

GNR 4-4-2 (Ivatt, Class C1)
251/3251-2800 .... NRM

NER 0-8-0 (Raven, Class Q6)
2238-3395/63395 .... NYMR

NER 0-8-0 (Raven, Class Q7)
901-3460/63460 .... NYMR

GCR 2-8-0 (Robinson, Class O4)
5102-3509/63601 .... DR

NER 0-6-0 (Worsdell, Class J21)
876-5033/65033 .... Beamish

NBR 0-6-0 (Reid, Class J36)
9673-5243/65243 Maude .... SRPS

GER 0-6-0 (Worsdell, Class J15)
7564/65462 .... NNR

GER 0-6-0 (Holden, Class J17)
8217-5567/65567 .... NRM

NER 0-6-0 (Worsdell, Class J27)
2392-5894/65894 .... NYMR

Ministry of Supply 0-6-0ST (Class J94)
8077/68077 .... KWVR
8078/68078 .... SRC

GER 0-4-0ST (Neilson & Co., Class Y5)
229 .... NWSM

NER 0-4-0T (Worsdell, Class Y7)
985-8088/68088 .... GCR
1310 .... MR

NBR 0-4-0ST (Drummond, Class Y9)
9042-8095/68095 .... LMPM

LNER 0-4-0T (Sentinel, Class Y1)
59-8153/68153 .... MR

LNER 0-4-0T (Holden, Class J69)
7087-8633/68633 .... NRM

GNR 0-6-0ST (Ivatt, Class J52)
4247-8846/68846 .... NRM

NER 0-6-0T (Worsdell, Class J72)
69023 Joem .... NYMR

GNR 0-6-2T (Gresley, Class N2)
4744-9523/69523 .... GCR

GER 0-6-2T (Hill, Class N7)
999E-7999-9621/69621 .... STVR

NER 2-2-4T (Class X1)
66/1478-66 Aerolite .... NRM

NER 2-4-0 (Fletcher, Class 910)
910/910 .... NRM

S&DR 0-6-0 (Bouch, Class 1001)
1275/1275 .... DNRM

NER 2-4-0 (Tennant, Class E5)
1463/1463 .... DNRM

NER 4-4-0 (Worsdell, Class D17)
1621/1621 .... NRM

GNR 4-4-2 (Ivatt, Class C2)
990/3990 Henry Oakley .... NRM

GNR 4-4-2 (Stirling 'Single')
1 .... NRM

S&DR 0-4-0 (Stephenson)
1 Locomotion .... DNRM

S&DR 0-6-0
Derwent .... DNRM

BRITISH RAILWAYS STANDARD LOCOMOTIVES

'Britannia' 4-6-2 (Class 7P)
70000 Britannia .... S'TWN
70013 Oliver Cromwell .... BSM

Class 8P 4-6-2
71000 Duke of Gloucester .... GCR

Class 5MT 4-6-0
73050 City of Peterborough ..'................... NVR
73082 Camelot .... BR
73096 .... MHR
73129 .... MRC
73156 .... ELR

Class 4MT 4-6-0
75014 .... NYMR
75027 .... BR
75029 The Green Knight .... ESR
75069 .... SVR
75078 .... KWVR
75079 .... PVR

Class 4MT 2-6-0
76017 .... MHR
76077 .... BI
76079 .... SRM
76084 .... South Leverton

Class 2MT 2-6-0
78018 .... Henry Boot & Co., Darlington
78019 .... SVR
78022 .... KWVR
78059 .... BR

Class 4MT 2-6-4T
80002 .... KWVR
80064 .... BR
80072 .... BI
80078 .... SW
80079 .... SVR
80080 .... MRC
80097 .... ELR
80098 .... MRC
80100 .... BR
80104 .... SW
80105 .... SRPS
80135 .... NYMR
80136 .... NSR
80150 .... BI
80151 .... STVR

Class 9F 2-10-0
92134 .... Shipyard Services, Essex
92203 Black Prince .... ESR
92207 Morning Star .... ELR
92212 .... GCR
92214 .... PR
92219 .... PR
92220 Evening Star .... NRM
92240 .... BR
92245 .... BI

WAR DEPARTMENT LOCOMOTIVES

Class WD 2-10-0
600 Gordon .... SVR
73652-90775/3652 .... MHR
73675/3672 .... NYMR

Class WD 2-8-0
1931/5927-75927 .... KWVR

Class WD 0-6-0ST
190 Castle Hedingham .... CVR
191/23 Holman F Stephens .... KESR
192/92 Waggoner .... Museum of Army Transport
193 Shropshire .... LR
194 Cumbria .... LHR
196 Errol Lonsdale .... MHR
197/25 Northiam .... KESR
198/98 Royal Engineer .... MoD, Long Marston
200/24 William H Austen .... KESR

127

BIBLIOGRAPHY

GWR Engines; Names, Numbers & Classes .... David & Charles (Repr. GWR).
Halls, Granges & Manors at Work .... Michael Rutherford (Ian Allan, 1985).
LSWR Locomotives: The Drummond Classes .... D.G. Bradley (Wild Swan, 1986).
Bulleid, Last Giant of Steam .... Sean Day-Lewis (George Allen & Unwin, 1964).
Bulleid's Pacifics .... D.W. Winkworth (George Allen & Unwin, 1974).
Bulleid Locomotives .... Brian Haresnape (Ian Allan, 1977).
Southern Steam .... O.S. Nock (Pan/David & Charles 1966).
William Stanier .... O.S. Nock (Ian Allan, 1964).
Stanier 4-6-0s of the LMS .... J.W.P. Rowledge & Brian Reed (David & Charles, 1977).
Stanier Pacifics at Work .... A.J. Powell (Ian Allan, 1986).
LMS Reflections .... Bob Essery & Nigel Harris (Silver Link, 1986).
An Illustrated History of LMS Locomotives: Volumes 1, 2 & 3 .... Bob Essery & David Jenkinson (OPC, 1981, 1985, 1986).
An Illustrated History of Midland Locomotives .... Bob Essery & David Jenkinson (Wild Swan, 1984).
The Power of the Duchesses .... David Jenkinson (OPC, 1979).
The Midland Railway .... C. Hamilton Ellis (Ian Allan, 1953).
Locomotives of Sir Nigel Gresley .... O.S. Nock (Railway Publishing Co., 1945).
East Coast Pacifics at Work .... P.N. Townend (Ian Allan, 1982).
LNER Reflections .... Nigel Harris (Ed) (Silver Link, 1985).
A History of the LNER .... Michael R. Bonavia (George Allen & Unwin, 1983).
Locomotives of the LNER .... Various Volumes (RCTS)
The abc of British Railways Locomotives (various editions) .... (Ian Allan)
The Pocket Encyclopaedia of British Steam Locomotives .... O.S. Nock (Blandford, 1964).
Steam Railways of Britain .... O.S. Nock (Blandford, 1967).
British Locomotives of the 20th Century: Volumes 1 & 2 .... O.S. Nock (PSL, 1983, 1984).
The British Steam Railway Locomotive: Volume 2 1925-1965 .... O.S. Nock (Ian Allan, 1965).
Locomotives of British Railways .... H.C. Casserley & L.L. Asher (Spring Books, 1961).
The Standard Steam Locomotives of British Railways .... Rodger Bradley (David & Charles 1984).
The Somerset & Dorset Railway .... Robin Atthill (Pan/David & Charles, 1967).
Industrial Steam Locomotives .... V.F. Hall (Moorland).
British Atlantic Locomotives .... C.J. Allan (Ian Allan, 1968).
What Happened to Steam? (various volumes) .... (Defiant)
British Railways Past & Present No. 1; Cumbria .... John Broughton & Nigel Harris (Silver Link, 1985).
Keighley & Worth Valley Railway Stockbook .... (KWVR, 1984).
A Century on Rails (Buckinghamshire Railway Centre Stockbook) .... Trevor Page (BRC, 1985).
History of Railways, Volumes 1 & 2 .... (New English Library).
Great Trains .... (New English Library).

Monthly journals & periodicals:
Railway World.
Railway Magazine.
Locomotives Illustrated. } .... Various issues, 1897–1987.
Trains Illustrated.
Steam World.
Steam Railway.